remember
LITTLE ROCK

remember

LITTLE ROCK

The Time, the People, the Stories

Paul Robert Walker

with a foreword by **Terrence J. Roberts,**
Ph.D., of the Little Rock Nine

NATIONAL
GEOGRAPHIC

WASHINGTON, D.C.

To the spirit, commitment, and courage of the Little Rock Nine.

STAFF FOR THIS BOOK
Suzanne Patrick Fonda, *Project Editor*
David M. Seager, *Art Director*
Callie Broaddus, *Associate Designer*
Lori Epstein, *Senior Photo Editor*
Paul Robert Walker, *Illustrations Editor*
Sven M. Dolling, *Map Research and Production*
Paige Towler, *Editorial Assistant*
Ruthie Thompson, *Production Designer*
Jennifer A. Thornton, *Managing Editor*
Grace Hill, *Associate Managing Editor*
R. Gary Colbert, *Production Director*
Lewis R. Bassford, *Production Manager*
Jennifer Hoff, *Manager, Production Services*

PUBLISHED BY THE NATIONAL GEOGRAPHIC SOCIETY
Gary E. Knell, *President and CEO*
John M. Fahey, *Chairman of the Board*
Melina Gerosa Bellows, *Chief Education Officer*
Declan Moore, *Chief Media Officer*
Hector Sierra, *Senior Vice President and General Manager, Book Division*

SENIOR MANAGEMENT TEAM, KIDS PUBLISHING AND MEDIA
Nancy Laties Feresten, *Senior Vice President;* Jennifer Emmett, *Vice President, Editorial Director, Kids Books;* Julie Vosburgh Agnone, *Vice President, Editorial Operations;* Rachel Buchholz, *Editor and Vice President,* NG Kids *magazine;* Michelle Sullivan, *Vice President, Kids Digital;* Eva Absher-Schantz, *Design Director;* Jay Sumner, *Photo Director;* Hannah August, *Marketing Director;* R. Gary Colbert, *Production Director*

DIGITAL
Anne McCormack, *Director;* Laura Goertzel, Sara Zeglin, *Producers;* Jed Winer, *Special Projects Assistant;* Emma Rigney, *Creative Producer;* Brian Ford, *Video Producer;* Bianca Bowman, *Assistant Producer;* Natalie Jones, *Senior Product Manager*

Text is set in ITC New Baskerville.
Display type is set in Template Gothic Bold.

ACKNOWLEDGMENTS
First and foremost, thanks to Terrence Roberts, whom I met in the grand foyer of Central High on the afternoon of the 50th Anniversary Celebration. Terrence quickly embraced this project, and I could not have imagined a better guide. Thanks also to Minnijean Brown Trickey and Gloria Ray Karlmark, who offered their support throughout the project, and to Ernest Green and Carlotta Walls LaNier, who read the manuscript and offered their insights. Working with these five members of the Little Rock Nine was an unexpected gift for which I will always be grateful.

I was also fortunate to learn from white students who attended Central in 1957. A great big thanks to Robin Woods Loucks, who not only shared her memories but, along with her husband, Harry, graciously opened their Little Rock home to me during an extended research trip. Thanks also to Ralph Brodie, whom I met in a third-floor hallway of Central High; to Glennys Oakes Johns, Charles Oakley, and Steve Swafford, whom I interviewed in the same physics lab they shared with Ernest Green; and to Dent Gitchel, who offered his memories of the chili story.

Finally, a big thanks to the professionals who helped me research this story and obtain historic photographs: Laura Miller and Spirit Trickey-Rowan (Little Rock Central High National Historic Site); Tom Dillard and Geoffery Stark (Special Collections, University of Arkansas, Fayetteville); David Stricklin, Rhonda Stewart, and Charles Rodgers (Butler Center for Arkansas Studies); Russell Baker (Arkansas State History Commission); Stella Cameron (Central High School Library); Frank Fellone *(Arkansas Democrat-Gazette);* Brad Cook (Indiana University Archives); Denise King (Library of Congress), and authors Elizabeth Jacoway and Grif Stockley.

PHOTO CREDITS
Associated Press: 4–5, 11 (& back cover), 23, 43 (lower), back cover (lower right); Bettman/Corbis: cover, 20, 29, 30 (upper), 37 (upper), 42, 46, 48 (upper), 49, 51 (upper), 53 (upper), 55; Will Counts Collection, Indiana University Archives: 10, 13, 14, 28, 34 (upper), 41, 43 (upper); courtesy *Arkansas Democrat-Gazette:* 16, 18 (both), 27 (from Down from the Hills, by Orval Faubus), 31, 54 (upper, from Crisis at Central High, by Elizabeth Huckaby); courtesy Gloria Ray Karlmark: 54 (lower); courtesy Robin Woods Loucks: 35 (& back cover); from The Pix of '58 (Central High Yearbook): 36 (upper), 44 (both), 48 (lower), 51 (center & lower), 52 (both), 53 (lower); Getty Images: 38, 45; Library of Congress: 12, 17, 21, 37 (lower), 39 (& back cover); National Park Service/Little Rock Central High School National Historic Site: 8, 15; Larry Obsitnik Collection, Special Collections, University of Arkansas, Fayetteville, and *Arkansas Democrat-Gazette:* 19, 24 (& back cover), 25, 30 (lower), 34 (lower), 40 (lower & back cover); Special Collections, University of Arkansas, Fayetteville: 26, 40 (upper), 47; Jorunn Ricketts: 50 (from Tender Warriors, by Dorothy Sterling); Gertrude Samuels: 36 (lower, from Crisis at Central High, by Elizabeth Huckaby); Bob Trout: 33; Paul Robert Walker: 56.

COVER: *Central High student Hazel Bryan taunts Elizabeth Eckford in front of the school on September 4, 1957.*

TITLE PAGE: *U.S. soldiers from the 101st Airborne Division secure Park Street in front of Central High School on September 26, 1957.*

Sixteen-year-old Terrence Roberts faces the National Guard alone on the morning of September 4, 1957. Looking at this photo today, Dr. Roberts remarks, "I can't believe how calm I looked on the outside. I didn't feel calm inside."

Governor Faubus's decision to call out the Arkansas National Guard to keep me and eight other black students from attending Little Rock's Central High in 1957 was a personal affront. I loved school and wanted nothing more than to start my junior year with the least amount of fanfare. Sadly, that was not to be the case. I can still hear the roar of the mob when I recall that first day: the ear-splitting yells, the racist epithets, the mean-spirited remarks—it all comes back as if it were happening anew. In the midst of that turmoil I was outwardly calm, but inside I was a bundle of frightened nerves, wondering if I would live to see tomorrow.

I had chosen to be one of the first black students at Central High because it seemed so necessary to change the way black people were treated in Little Rock. Socially, culturally, politically, and—until 1954—legally, we were locked out of the mainstream of life. Racial oppression was like a lead blanket thrown over the heads of black people, weighing us down and making it extremely difficult to manage even the basic tasks of daily existence. Education was presented as the way out. "Get your education" were the words I heard most often growing up in Little Rock. My parents held education in high regard; my first grade teacher insisted that we students had to take control of our own learning, and other teachers in the all-black schools echoed this sentiment time and again.

I accepted that challenge and learned to appreciate what education could provide. It was clear that Central High, which was my neighborhood school, had the resources to add substantially to my growing storehouse of knowledge and information. It was equally clear that many white citizens in Little Rock would do all they could to interfere with my plans. According to their belief system, black children had no right to attend Central High.

As you read through this account of the year the nine of us spent at Central, and as you consider the physical and psychological abuse we encountered, you may wonder why on earth would we put ourselves through such an ordeal? While this is not an easy question to answer, there are three reasons that stand out in bold relief.

First, we were in the right; our cause was just and firmly grounded in the newly changed legal framework that outlawed segregated schools. Second, we were aware that hundreds of people before us had given their lives for the cause of equality. Saying no to this opportunity would have been the same as spitting on their graves. Third, we were able to make the daily decisions to return to the battlefield that Central became because we had the backing of the "village" of most black people in Little Rock and of those white people who were willing to face the social and economic sanctions imposed by their less charitable brethren.

In the pages that follow you will read about many of the people whose actions, either for good or bad, helped to shape the story of the Little Rock Nine. Paul Robert Walker has captured much of the pathos of that fateful year, and he provides a clear and accurate account of the events.

Terrence J. Roberts, Ph.D.

Elizabeth Eckford ignores the mob and reporters around her as she waits for a bus to take her home after being denied entrance to Central High School on September 4, 1957. The man with the bow tie is Dr. Benjamin Fine, education editor for the *New York Times*, who dared to show concern for Elizabeth.

september 4, 1957

As Elizabeth Eckford ironed the black and white dress she had made for her first day of school, her little brother turned on the television set. The TV announcer spoke of a large crowd in front of Central High School, just two miles from Elizabeth's house. It was about 7 a.m. on Wednesday, September 4, 1957, and the crowd had gathered because Elizabeth and eight other black students were scheduled to enter Central High that morning. They would be the first black students to go to school with whites in Little Rock—one of the great tests of school integration in the South.

Two days earlier, on Labor Day, the last day before the new school year began, Governor Orval Faubus had ordered the Arkansas National Guard to surround the school "to maintain or restore the peace." The governor claimed that the soldiers would not act "as segregationists or integrationists." He feared there would be violence if the black students tried to enter the school: "It is my opinion—yes even a conviction, that it will not be possible to restore or to maintain order and protect the lives and property of the citizens if forcible integration is carried out tomorrow."

Uncertain what the governor's action meant, the superintendent of the Little Rock School District asked the black students to stay home on Tuesday, September 3, while almost 1,900 white students got their books and class schedules. Now, on September 4, Elizabeth and the others were preparing to join them.

"Turn that TV off!" snapped Elizabeth's mother, who was making breakfast. Both she and her husband had opposed their daughter's plans to enroll at Central, but Elizabeth had convinced them that everything would be all right. They were much more nervous about the day ahead than she was. "I was more concerned about what I would wear, whether we could finish my dress in time," Elizabeth recalled. "When the governor went on television and announced that he had called out the Arkansas National Guard, I thought that he had done this to insure the protection of all the students."

Elizabeth would be a junior. She was a quiet, studious young woman who wanted to be a lawyer. One reason she applied to attend Central was to take a speech class that

Governor Orval Faubus

would help in her future law career. The all-black high school in Little Rock, Horace Mann High, was a good school compared with most other black schools in the South, but it did not offer as many challenging classes. Along with basic subjects such as math and English, Horace Mann offered laundry, food service, and other classes that would prepare black students for the jobs open to them. Elizabeth and the other courageous students who would become known as the Little Rock Nine had higher ambitions.

Although Elizabeth didn't know it, the nine black students were supposed to meet that morning at a corner two blocks from the school, so they could be escorted by a group of ministers, black and white. This plan had been arranged late the night before by Daisy Bates, president of the Arkansas Branch of the National Association for the Advancement of Colored People (NAACP). Mrs. Bates tried to contact all the students, but Elizabeth's family never got the message because they did not have a telephone. So Elizabeth took the city bus and then walked to school alone.

Another of the Nine, Terrence Roberts—a tall, thin junior—did have a phone, but for some unknown reason he never got a call either. He also went to school alone. Terrence lived closer than Elizabeth—just six blocks away—so he walked. "After break-fast and last minute preparations for the anticipated first day," he wrote, "I tucked a sharpened #2 pencil behind one ear, packed up my notebooks and marched off to school." Like Elizabeth, he believed the National Guardsmen were there to protect him.

Elizabeth arrived first, getting off her bus two blocks from Central High. When she turned onto Park Street, she saw a large crowd gathered farther up the street, directly across from the school. "As I walked on," she remembered, "the crowd suddenly got very quiet." When she reached the corner of the school grounds at Park and 14th, a Guardsman pointed across Park toward the crowd. Elizabeth asked if he meant that she should cross the street and walk farther down, toward the front entrance, and he nodded yes.

"So I walked across the street, then someone shouted, 'Here she comes, get ready!' I moved away from the crowd on the sidewalk and into the street. If a mob came at me, I could then cross back over so the guards could protect me.

"The crowd moved in closer and then began to follow me, calling me names. I still wasn't afraid. Just a little bit nervous. Then my knees began to shake all of a sudden,

Terrence Roberts

12

and I wondered whether I could make it to the center entrance a block away. It was the longest block I ever walked in my life."

When Elizabeth reached the front entrance of the school, she approached a Guardsman who had let a number of white students pass. "He didn't move," she remembered. "When I tried to squeeze past him, he raised his rifle, and then the other guards moved in, and they raised their rifles. They glared at me with a mean look, and I was very frightened and didn't know what to do. I turned around, and the crowd came toward me. They moved closer and closer.

"I tried to see a friendly face somewhere in the mob—somebody who maybe would help. I looked into the face of an old woman, but when I looked at her again, she spat on me.

"I turned back to the guards, but their faces told me I wouldn't get any help from them. Then I looked down the block and saw a bench at the bus stop. I thought, 'If I can only get there, I will be safe.' I didn't know why the bench seemed a safe place to me, but I started walking toward it. I tried to close my mind to what they were shouting, and kept saying to myself, 'If I can only make it to the bench, I will be safe.'"

As Elizabeth walked toward the bench, a white student named Hazel Bryan walked directly behind her shouting with such anger that her contorted face—captured by two separate photographers at the same instant—became the image of racism seen around the world *(see front cover)*.

Hazel, who left Central to attend an all-white school, later explained that her church experiences led her to do what she did that day. "I felt very religious at that time. I attended church every Sunday morning and night, as well as Wednesday nights. While no one at church said that we should protest school integration, we got the feeling that it would be a good thing to do." In fact, many white ministers preached that segregation was "God's way" as they interpreted the Bible. Other ministers believed the Bible taught equality for all races.

Finally, Elizabeth reached the bench at the bus stop on the corner of Park and 16th Streets. "I don't think I could have gone another step," she remembered. "I sat down, and the mob hollered, 'Drag her over to this tree!' Just then a white man sat down beside me, put his arm around me, and patted my shoulder. He raised my chin and said, 'Don't let them see you cry.'"

Dr. Benjamin Fine

The white man who sat beside Elizabeth was Dr. Benjamin Fine, the education editor for the *New York Times*. A few days later, he told Daisy Bates that he had reached out to Elizabeth because she reminded him of his own 15-year-old daughter back in New York.

Several other people tried to help Elizabeth on that bench as the mob surrounded her. L.C. Bates, Daisy's husband, sat down and showed her that he had a gun. He offered to take her home, but she politely declined. She had been the last of the black students accepted at Central and had never met Daisy or L.C. Although she knew that he was publisher of a newspaper for the Little Rock black community, Elizabeth would never go anywhere with a man she didn't know personally.

Terrence Roberts arrived at school a few minutes after Elizabeth, and like her, he faced the Guardsmen alone, with the crowd swarming around him. "Up close the surly crowd was frightening," he remembered. "I was surrounded immediately by a corps of reporters and photographers as members of the mob behind them jeered and shouted obscenities. I alternately responded to questions from the media represent-atives and attempted to walk through the line of guardsmen. After a few tries it became apparent that the guard's primary assignment was to keep me out of school."

When a newsman told Terrence that another black student was sitting on the bench down the street, he made his way past the reporters and asked Elizabeth if she wanted to walk home with him. She declined, just as she had declined the offer from L.C. Bates. She later told Terrence that she was afraid the mob might follow them, and she still would have had to find a way home.

By this time, a white woman named Grace Lorch had arrived. She screamed at the mob, "Leave this child alone! Why are you tormenting her? Six months from now, you will hang your heads in shame."

"Another nigger lover," the mob shouted back. "Get out of here!"

Mrs. Lorch told Terrence that she would stay with Elizabeth until the bus came. Although neither Elizabeth nor Terrence knew who this kind white woman was, she

L.C. Bates, husband of Daisy Bates and publisher of a black newspaper called the *State Press,* sits beside Elizabeth at the bus stop. He had left his wife in the car outside the school and rushed to Elizabeth's side after hearing about her ordeal on the radio. He clutches a gun in his pocket.

Integration supporter Grace Lorch (right) argues with a protester in the crowd outside Central High on the morning of September 4, 1957. Mrs. Lorch helped Elizabeth get on the bus and then got off after a few blocks. Instead of going home, Elizabeth rode the bus to the Arkansas School for the Blind and Deaf Negro, where her mother was working.

was deeply committed to the cause of racial justice. Her husband—also white—was a mathematics professor at the all-black Philander Smith College in Little Rock. Two years earlier the Little Rock School Board had denied Mrs. Lorch's request to allow her 11-year-old daughter to go to the all-black elementary school in their neighborhood. It was no accident that the ardent integrationist was there that day.

Confident that Mrs. Lorch would look after Elizabeth, Terrence headed for home. "I had walked perhaps half a block," he recalled, "when I heard footsteps behind me, and turned around to see a lone, white male adult coming toward me. I assumed a karate stance in anticipation of a fight when he waved his hand and said that he was a friend. He apologized on behalf of the people who were gathered around the school and said he wanted me to know that not all white people were opposed to desegregating Central High. About that time my dad walked up. He had seen the increasing chaos via live television coverage and was coming to escort me home. We thanked the man whose name I never knew, and we continued our walk home."

Melba Pattillo, a pretty junior who had a talent for writing, arrived with her mother around the same time as Elizabeth. Mrs. Pattillo parked their car a few blocks from the school. Looking for the other black students and the ministers, they were caught in the crowd in front of Central, where the mob was chanting: "Two, four, six, eight, we ain't gonna integrate!" Standing on her tiptoes, Melba could see Elizabeth facing off with the National Guard and watched as she walked toward the bench, with "people yelping at her heels, like mad dogs." Melba and her mother suddenly realized that they, too, were in the middle of a violent mob.

"Ever so slowly, we eased our way backward through the crowd," Melba wrote, "being careful not to attract attention. But a white man clawed at me, grabbing my sleeve and yelling, 'We got us a nigger right here!'...Somehow I managed to scramble away. As a commotion began building around us, Mother took my arm, and we moved fast, sometimes crouching to avoid attracting more attention."

Heading down the block, Melba looked back to see four white men following behind, with others joining them. Although Melba did not yet have her driver's license, her mother handed her the car keys and told her to leave without her if she had to. Melba refused to leave her mother, who was moving more slowly in high-heeled shoes.

"The men chasing us were joined by another carrying a rope," she remembered. "At times, our pursuers were so close I could look back and see the anger in their eyes. Mama's pace slowed, and one man came close enough to touch her. He grabbed for her arm but instead tugged at her blouse. The fabric ripped, and he fell backward. Mama stepped out of her high-heeled shoes, leaving them behind, her pace quickening in stocking feet.

"One of the men closest to me swung at me with a large tree branch but missed. I felt even more panic rise up in my throat....As I turned the corner, our car came into sight, I ran hard—faster than ever before—unlocked the door, and jumped in."

Melba's mother managed to get in just ahead of her pursuers, and Melba threw the gearshift into reverse and drove backwards down the street as fast as she could. As she slowed down to back around the corner, "one of the men caught up and pounded his fists on the hood of the car, while another threw a brick at the windshield.

"Turning left, we gained speed as we drove through a hail of shouts and stones and glaring faces. But I knew I would make it because the car was moving fast and Mama was with me."

While Melba and her mother were making their escape, Mrs. Lorch and Dr. Fine took Elizabeth across the street to a drugstore, so they could call a cab for her. "I remained on the sidewalk with Elizabeth," Dr. Fine remembered, "while Mrs. Lorch tried to enter the drugstore. But the hoodlums slammed the door on her and wouldn't let her in....They closed in on her saying, 'Get out of here you bitch!'"

Melba Pattillo

Beverly Burks

Arkansas State Police Sergeant L.E. Gwyn displays weapons confiscated or found in the Central High area from September 3 to 5, the first days of mob activity around the school.

A sophomore named Beverly Burks later told agents of the Federal Bureau of Investigation (FBI) that she was in the drugstore that morning and saw several students with weapons, including a couple of switchblades, "a belt with some tacks or nails in it...to wrap around his fist," and a large pocket knife. Three older boys who were not students had tire irons in their cars, and one of them told Beverly "he would like to get hold of one of the Negroes to use [it]."

Finally, the bus arrived and Mrs. Lorch and Elizabeth got on, with the grey-haired Mrs. Lorch threatening several young men if they didn't get out of the way. "I am just aching to punch someone in the nose," she said. "You stand there and you will get your nose punched in."

Now the mob turned on Dr. Fine, calling him "a dirty New York Jew" and threatening to cut off his private parts. "During all this time," he recalled, "the National Guardsmen made no effort to protect Elizabeth or to help me. Instead they threatened to have me arrested—for inciting to riot."

Elizabeth Eckford, Terrence Roberts, and Melba Pattillo had the worst experiences that morning, but the other members of the Little Rock Nine—Ernest Green, the only senior of the group; juniors Minnijean Brown and Thelma Mothershed; and sophomores Gloria Ray, Carlotta Walls, and Jefferson Thomas—were also turned away. There was a tenth student, Jane Hill, but after the morning's events, she decided to return to Horace Mann.

These seven students gathered at the corner of Park and 12th Streets, two blocks from the school, and walked with a group of adults, including Mrs. Bates, two black ministers, three white ministers, and the adult son of one of the white ministers. When the group approached the same corner of the school grounds where Elizabeth had first encountered the National Guard, they were met by Colonel Marion Johnson, who blocked their path with a big wooden baton. "This school is off limits to Negro students," he said, "and Negro schools are off limits to white students."

Members of the Little Rock Nine who walked with the ministers on September 4 are turned away by the Arkansas National Guard. In the foreground, left to right, are Ernest Green, Thelma Mothershed, Gloria Ray, Carlotta Walls, and Minnijean Brown. Jefferson Thomas (not pictured) was also with them. The tall girl next to Ernest is Jane Hill, a black student who decided to return to Horace Mann High rather than try to register at Central High.

One of the black ministers, Reverend Harry Bass, asked Colonel Johnson if he was acting on orders from Governor Faubus, and the colonel replied that he was. This was an important statement. For the first time it was crystal clear that the governor had ordered the troops to do more than keep the peace: They were there to keep the black students out.

Confronted with the stern-faced colonel and 300 National Guardsmen, the group decided to retreat for the day and go to the office of the school superintendent. He was out, so they went to the office of the federal district attorney, where several of the adults and students gave statements to FBI agents. The federal lawmen had been sent to Little Rock to investigate efforts by segregationists to interfere with the school board's plan to comply with integration ordered by federal courts. Now it was clear that the segregationists had a powerful ally: Governor Orval Faubus.

September 4, 1957, would go down in history as one of the darkest days in American racial relations, and all of the Little Rock Nine—especially Elizabeth Eckford—would carry the emotional pain of that day throughout their lives. It was ugly, but it was only the beginning of the Battle of Little Rock.

Separate drinking fountains were just one of many ways that Jim Crow laws kept the races apart. In the early 1950s state-legislated segregation was still widespread, not only in the former Confederacy but also in a number of bordering states.

jim crow & orval faubus

The Little Rock Nine grew up in the Jim Crow South—a place and time that made blacks second-class citizens. Blacks and whites went to separate schools and churches, drank from separate water fountains, used separate public restrooms, ate at separate restaurants, stayed at separate hotels or private homes, and rode in separate railroad cars. Blacks sat in the back of public buses and in the balconies of movie theaters. They could be brutally attacked by whites at any time, and there was little chance that the attackers would be convicted of a crime.

Jim Crow was a character in minstrel shows before the Civil War. In these musicals white performers would blacken their faces and dance a silly jig to a song called "Jump Jim Crow." The Jim Crow character became a symbol of the racist idea that blacks were inferior. The term "Jim Crow" came to refer to all the laws and customs that deprived blacks of their civil rights.

After the Civil War, there was a brief time of equality for newly freed slaves, but every state in the South—and some in the North—passed Jim Crow laws that kept the races apart. The true Jim Crow era began in 1896, when the U.S. Supreme Court decided that it was legal to have "separate but equal" facilities for blacks and whites. The original court decision (Plessy v. Ferguson) dealt with blacks riding in separate railroad cars, but in the South it was applied to every public place, including schools.

During the 1930s, lawyers from the NAACP began to fight segregation in education. The turning point in this legal battle came in May 1954, when the U.S. Supreme Court ruled that the idea of "separate but equal" did not apply to public schools. The Court said that even if the buildings and other physical aspects were the same, "to separate [black children] from others of similar age and qualifications solely because of their race generates a feeling of inferiority as to their status in the community that may affect their hearts and minds in a way unlikely ever to be undone."

Jim Crow

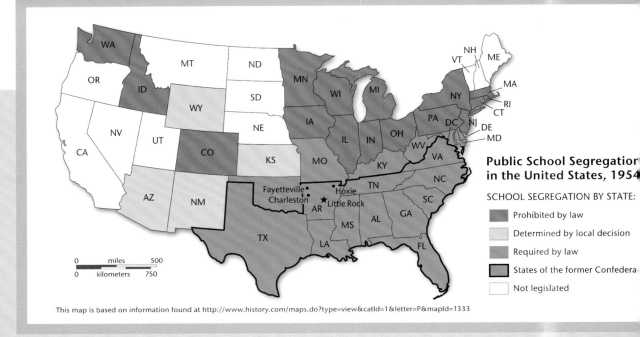

Public School Segregation in the United States, 1954

SCHOOL SEGREGATION BY STATE:

- Prohibited by law
- Determined by local decision
- Required by law
- States of the former Confedera
- Not legislated

This map is based on information found at http://www.history.com/maps.do?type=view&catId=1&letter=P&mapId=1333

As this map shows, at the time of the *Brown* decision in 1954, 17 states and the District of Columbia had laws requiring public school segregation, and 4 others had laws permitting segregation by local school districts. Other states either had laws forbidding school segregation or had no laws about it.

This ruling, *Brown v. Board of Education of Topeka, Kansas,* sent shock waves across the former Confederacy and bordering states such as Kansas, Missouri, and Kentucky. At this time, 17 states plus the District of Columbia had laws requiring segregated public schools and 4 others had laws allowing segregated schools. Every state and community scrambled to understand how the ruling would affect them.

The Court ordered that integration must proceed "with all deliberate speed." A year later, a second ruling called *Brown II* made clear that "deliberate speed" would depend on the local situation. It was up to local federal courts to decide whether each school district was moving fast enough.

In a number of Deep South states, including Georgia, Mississippi, and Alabama, white segregationists formed Citizens Councils to fight integration. The Virginia state legislature called for "massive resistance" against integration and passed a series of laws that closed many public schools rather than integrate them. In early 1956 one hundred senators and congressmen from the former Confederate states signed a document called "The Southern Manifesto," which claimed that the Supreme Court had no right to interfere with education in the states. Referring to the *Brown* rulings, it said: "This unwarranted exercise of power by the Court, contrary to the Constitution, is creating chaos and confusion in the States principally affected. It is destroying the amicable relations between the white and Negro races that have been created through 90 years of patient effort by the good people of both races. It has planted hatred and suspicion where there has been heretofore friendship and understanding." The concepts of "amicable relations" and "friendship and understanding" between the races in the Jim Crow South were favorite themes embraced by segregationists. Few blacks agreed.

Although all Arkansas senators and congressmen signed the Southern Manifesto, no one expected massive resistance in the state. The medical and law schools at the University of Arkansas had been integrated in 1948, and the Little Rock Public Library was integrated three years later. Two school districts in northwestern Arkansas, Fayetteville and Charleston, integrated in 1954—the first in the former Confederacy to do so. Both of these districts are in the Ozark Mountain region of northwest Arkansas, where there were few blacks. It was cheaper for these districts to let black students go to local public schools than to continue to transport them by bus to an all-black school in a bigger city. These first steps of school integration attracted little notice.

The Arkansas situation shifted dramatically in the summer of 1955, when a school district in the small town of Hoxie, in northeastern Arkansas, integrated peacefully. *Life* magazine published photos of black and white students together. To many Americans, these photos offered a promise that blacks and whites in the South could live together in equality. To the segregationists, they were a call to action. Hoxie was in an area near the Mississippi River where cotton farming was still the main economic activity, and the white farmers wanted to maintain control over their black workforce.

Segregationists from other parts of Arkansas joined hundreds of local whites in protesting integration and forced the schools to close for awhile. FBI agents investigated the disturbances, and a federal court ruled that the Hoxie School District must integrate without interference. The segregationists were defeated for a time, but they were now organized under a new leader, Jim Johnson—a tall, handsome lawyer and powerful public speaker.

Johnson wrote an amendment to the state constitution that would require Arkansas to "pass

The three NAACP attorneys who won the *Brown* case pose on the steps of the U.S. Supreme Court, in Washington, D.C. Left to right, they are George E.C. Hayes, Thurgood Marshall, and James M. Nabrit.

23

The popularity of segregationist Jim Johnson, pictured campaigning for governor in the summer of 1956, made Orval Faubus realize that he would have to adopt a segregationist position if he wanted to win the Democratic primary. Many years later Faubus admitted that Johnson had shown him the key issue that made Faubus a winner in Arkansas politics.

laws opposing in every Constitutional manner the un-Constitutional desegregation decisions of...the United States Supreme Court." The idea behind this amendment was that the Supreme Court did not have the right to tell Arkansas what to do with its education system, and the state had the right to nullify, or ignore, the decision of the Court. Johnson traveled from town to town, giving fiery speeches and gathering signatures of support for his amendment.

Jim Johnson challenged Governor Orval Faubus for the Democratic nomination in the spring of 1956. At this time in Arkansas and throughout the South the Democratic candidate for governor usually won the general election. So the real election that year was the Democratic primary between Faubus and Johnson. The segregationist leader accused Faubus of being part of a communist plot to weaken the South by mixing races: "Don't you know that the communist plan for more than fifty years has been to destroy southern civilization, one of the last patriotic and Christian strongholds, by mongrelization [race mixing], and our negroes are being exploited by them to affect their purposes?"

Until this time Orval Faubus had been considered a moderate in race relations. He was from a poor family in the hill country of northwestern Arkansas, and he first won election by appealing to poorer people, including blacks. Once elected, he brought more blacks into the Democratic party and opened more jobs for them in state government. Prior to the Central High School crisis, the Little Rock bus system and parks were both integrated peacefully under his administration. He had not interfered with the efforts to integrate schools in Hoxie or other small towns.

At the time, an Arkansas governor served a two-year term, so right after the election he had to start running for reelection. Johnson made school integration the number-one issue, so like any good politician, Faubus took a poll to see what the citizens thought. It's unclear who he polled—certainly few blacks, if any—but the results showed that 85 percent of Arkansas voters were against school integration. Faced with strong opposition from Johnson and the results of his own poll, Faubus promised: "No school district will be forced to mix the races as long as I am governor of Arkansas."

Faubus won the election in November 1956, but the voters approved Johnson's amendment to the state constitution. They also approved two more moderate laws sponsored by Faubus that would maintain segregation. A few months later the Arkansas legislature passed four other pro-segregation laws, putting federal and Arkansas law in direct conflict. Faubus knew that federal law canceled out state laws in this situation, but he also knew that the voters who reelected him did not want integration.

Despite the growing resistance to integration, the Little Rock School Board, in compliance with the federal courts, continued their plan to integrate Central High in the fall of 1957. This was the first step in a six-year plan to integrate all of the city's public schools. School Superintendent Virgil Blossom admitted to whites that the plan provided "the least amount of integration over the longest possible period." Even so, it was a faster effort than most school districts in other large Southern cities were willing to attempt.

At first about 80 black students applied to attend Central High School. This was a relatively small percentage of the more than 500 black students who lived in the Central attendance area, but it was too many for Blossom and the school board. Blossom asked the principals of the black schools to discourage some students based on their records. Eventually, the number of "finalists" was reduced to 17. Blossom and the other officials emphasized the high academic standards of Central High, the stress the black students would face, and the fact they would not be allowed to participate in extracurricular activities. This meant they could not play sports, participate in the band, or join any clubs. Eight of the 17 dropped out, leaving only the Little Rock Nine—all excellent students who came from solid, supportive families.

In the summer of 1957, as the opening day of school approached, Johnson's segregationist organization carried out a telephone campaign to influence Governor Faubus and intimidate Superintendent Blossom, who received threats to himself, his wife, and his daughters. These calls disturbed Blossom so much that he began to look for a way out. How could the school board postpone integration without disobeying federal

A harried looking Virgil Blossom rushes out of the U.S. District Attorney's office in Little Rock on September 5, 1957. The superintendent had taken part in a discussion about legal options open to the school board in the face of Governor Faubus's decision to use the Arkansas National Guard to prevent integration.

L.C. and Daisy Bates show detectives a partly burned cross—a symbol of the white supremacist Ku Klux Klan—planted in their front yard. In late August 1957 a rock with the note "STONE THIS TIME. THE NEXT WILL BE DYNAMITE. KKK" had shattered their front window.

law? Faubus also wanted a way out, and the two men agreed to find a private citizen who would sue the school board to stop integration.

On Tuesday, August 27, one week before school was to begin, Mary Thomason filed a suit in a local court asking to postpone integration of Central High because of threats of violence. Mrs. Thomason was the secretary of a segregationist organization called the Mothers League of Little Rock Central High School. Thomason, one of the few league members who actually had a child at Central, testified that she had heard "rumors from a filling [gas] station operator...that there was a possibility of shotguns or shooting in Central High if the colored children entered." She had also heard rumors of "gangs of white children and gangs of colored children being formed with a view to some sort of violence."

Governor Faubus also testified to the danger, saying there would be "rioting and bloodshed if the city program was put into effect." He told the court that he had talked with federal authorities, and "the federal government would not intervene." By this, Faubus meant that the federal government would not help the local or state authorities if there were violence.

The local judge granted Mrs. Thomason's request that integration be postponed, but the case was immediately appealed to a federal court. By this time, the regular federal judge in Arkansas had taken himself off the case because he was afraid it would hurt his career, so the case was heard by Judge Ronald Davies, a no-nonsense Northerner who had just arrived from North Dakota. To Davies the case was clear. The federal court had ordered integration, and he saw no reason to stop it. On Saturday morning, August 31, he overruled the lower court and ordered integration at Central High to continue as planned.

School was scheduled to begin Tuesday, September 3,

the day after Labor Day. Through that hot, muggy weekend, Governor Faubus stayed in the Governor's Mansion in Little Rock, about a mile and a half from Central High, trying to decide what to do. He was in a corner. The federal court had ordered integration, but the federal government would offer him no support to prevent violence. His poll and the results of the last election had showed him that most white citizens of Arkansas were against integration, and he believed there was real danger from protesters in Little Rock.

He had received many calls warning him about caravans of armed men heading for Little Rock to fight integration. A close friend of Faubus named Jimmy Karam, who was a segregationist, stayed at the mansion and screened the governor's calls so that he only heard from people who warned of violence. "All the people he thought was calling him," said Karam, "was everybody that thought just one way...'There's going to be blood in the streets.' Oh yes. That's all he heard."

Jim Johnson, who organized the phone calls, later admitted, "There wasn't any caravan. But we made Orval believe it. We said, 'They're lining up. They're coming in droves.'…The only weapon we had was to leave the impression the sky was going to fall." Despite Johnson's admission that he was bluffing about the caravans, there is evidence that some armed men did head for Little Rock. It was not the big organized caravans that Faubus feared, but the threat of violence was real—as the Little Rock Nine discovered on September 4.

After struggling all weekend over what action to take, Governor Faubus ordered the Arkansas National Guard to surround Central High School on the night of Monday, Labor Day, September 2. His exact orders that night are unclear, but by the next night he had definitely ordered the Guard to keep the black students out. It was a decision that would make him a hero to segregationists and a villain to integrationists and others who believed that federal law must be obeyed. The state of Arkansas was now in direct defiance of United States law, and the world waited to see what would happen next.

YOU SURE OF WHAT YOU SEE OUT THERE GOVERNOR?

This political cartoon from the *Arkansas Gazette* captures a key issue in the Little Rock conflict. Editor Harry Ashmore, who won a Pulitzer Prize for his editorials on the story, believed Faubus created the crisis by calling out the Guard without real evidence of violence. The truth is more complicated.

Alex Wilson, editor of the *Memphis Tri-State Defender*, is brutally attacked by the mob outside Central High on September 23, 1957. A fellow black newsman who was also attacked recalled, "During all that beating, Alex never let go of his hat."

september 23, 1957

After their attempt to enter Central High School on September 4 was blocked, the Little Rock Nine stayed out of school for almost three weeks while Governor Faubus battled with the federal government. The National Guard remained at Central High during this time.

The Nine studied together and had tutors from Philander Smith College, but it was difficult being out of school while their white classmates were learning. "I knew that going to Central I would have to continue to do well," recalled Carlotta Walls, "because in a sense I was representing a lot of other colored kids. I could learn as well as the next kid. I knew that. So every day that went by, I was getting further and further behind....I figured whenever we got back in school, I was going to have to not only be twice as good as that white kid, I was going to have to be the Super Negro."

On September 14, Governor Faubus met for more than two hours with President Dwight D. Eisenhower in Newport, Rhode Island, where the President was vacationing. Although they officially called the meeting "friendly and constructive," nothing was accomplished. Faubus promised the President that he would work for integration if the government would give him a "cooling-off period." The President promised nothing, but said, "Good luck to you and I hope it all works out all right."

The legal showdown came on Friday, September 20, in the crowded Little Rock courtroom of Judge Ronald Davies. According to one eyewitness, the hallway outside the courtroom "looked like something out of a Hollywood premier....The cameras whirred and flashbulbs flashed when the principals of the drama went out of the courtroom and into the floodlights."

There were two basic issues in the case: 1) Did the federal court have jurisdiction (authority) over a governor acting as commander-in-chief of the state militia? 2) Was Governor

Governor Faubus shakes hands with President Eisenhower after their meeting in Newport, Rhode Island, on September 14, 1957. Despite the smiles, their talks resolved nothing.

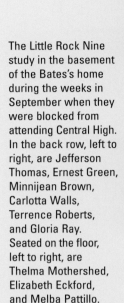

The Little Rock Nine study in the basement of the Bates's home during the weeks in September when they were blocked from attending Central High. In the back row, left to right, are Jefferson Thomas, Ernest Green, Minnijean Brown, Carlotta Walls, Terrence Roberts, and Gloria Ray. Seated on the floor, left to right, are Thelma Mothershed, Elizabeth Eckford, and Melba Pattillo.

Faubus using the Arkansas National Guard to defy a federal court order? Faubus claimed that he was using the troops not to defy the order but to prevent violence that would have occurred if the black students had entered the school.

After listening to two hours of arguments, Judge Davies ruled that the court did have jurisdiction. At this point, the lawyers for Governor Faubus walked out of the court—a dramatic way of saying they refused to accept the judge's ruling and would appeal to a higher court.

Faubus was in the Governor's Mansion, a mile away. According to a reporter who was with him that day, when he heard that his lawyers had left the court, he began writing a statement to the people of Arkansas that began with the words: "Now begins the crucifixion.…"

The governor believed that Judge Davies had decided how he would rule before the trial, and the evidence suggests Faubus was right. Although the FBI had interviewed more than 200 witnesses, the judge heard only 10: 8 white adults and 2 of the Little Rock Nine—Ernest Green and Elizabeth Eckford. The adults testified that there were no threats of violence, and Elizabeth and Ernest both said that they were not physically harmed. No one asked about emotional harm or the fear of being surrounded by a mob. Judge Davies had an FBI report in his possession that indicated some threats of violence were real, but he did not refer to it during the hearing.

As expected, Davies ruled that Governor Faubus had interfered with the court-approved integration plan. "It is [clear] from testimony here today that there would

Judge Ronald Davies

have been no violence in carrying out the plan of integration," he said, "and that there has been no violence." That evening, Faubus ordered the National Guard to leave the school. The next morning, he left the state for the Southern Governors Conference in Georgia.

With the Guard gone, Little Rock Mayor Woodrow Mann promised that the city police would keep the peace when the black students returned to the school on the 23rd. "The eyes of the nation and the world will be on Little Rock Monday and in the period immediately following....Military force will be at an end. The maintenance of law and order will now be where it belongs, in the hands of local law enforcement authorities and citizens of this community."

It was a reasonable idea, but these were not reasonable times.

The Little Rock Nine attempted to enter Central again on Monday, September 23. This time, they all met at the Bates's home. Some of the students' parents were able to stay, while others had to go to work after dropping their children off. There were many reporters there, too—both black and white.

The announcer on the radio spoke of a large mob gathered outside Central. Mrs. Bates recalled hearing on-the-street interviews with hate-filled comments such as, "Just let those niggers show up! Just let 'em try!" and "We won't stand for our schools being integrated. If we let 'em in, next thing they'll be marrying our daughters."

Looking back, it seems amazing that Daisy Bates and the students' parents allowed the Nine to go to school that day, but they all believed deeply in the cause of

Before classes on September 11, 1957, white students put on an informal street dance outside Central High for reporters and photographers, who were looking for a story during the time the Little Rock Nine stayed out of school.

integration, and they hoped the Little Rock police would protect them. Daisy Bates remembered two of the parents praying in her living room. She was not religious herself, but she found herself praying, too.

The students went in two cars, one driven by an NAACP official and the other by a young, black lawyer. Mrs. Bates went in one of the cars. They had been ordered by the police to enter the school through a side entrance near Park and 16th Streets, not far from the bench where Elizabeth Eckford had sat on September 4.

Daisy Bates had told three black reporters and a black photographer where the students would enter, and the four newsmen arrived about five minutes before the students. In full view of the Little Rock police, the angry mob attacked the four black men, kicking and striking at them with their fists. They grabbed the photographer's camera and smashed it on the ground, stomping it with their feet.

Three of the men escaped serious injury by running from their attackers, but one of them, Alex Wilson—a Marine Corps veteran and editor of a black newspaper in Memphis, Tennessee—took a terrible beating because he refused to run from the mob. He recalled his experience with a mix of sarcasm and painful honesty:

"I decided not to run. If I were to be beaten, I'd take it walking, if I could—not running. Members of the red-blooded democracy-loving mob acted swiftly. They sensed (I realize now) my determination. One hillbilly kicked at my left side. I broke the impact, not striking back. Another unleashed a looping right to my side. It grazed my jaw as I ducked. A brave Arkansas 'peckerwood' leaped upon my back, encircling my neck with his arm.

"Thanks to the Marine Corps training, I was able to shake him without sustaining injury. He backed away with a half-brick (with at least fifty persons behind him), yelling: 'Run, damn you, run!' I looked at him and at the brick, then picked up my hat, recreased it, and started walking again.

"A courageous white member of the mob at my back struck me on the back of my head. It was a hefty blow. To keep from falling, I lunged forward from the impact, to regain balance. I came upright near an auto, and looked into the tear-filled eyes of a White woman. Although there was sorrow in her eyes, I knew there would not be any help.

Photographer Will Counts of the *Arkansas Democrat* captures the action as police—with Assistant Chief Gene Smith in the right foreground—subdue a segregationist protester on September 23. Counts, a 26-year-old graduate of Central High, took some of the most dramatic photos of the Little Rock crisis.

"I walked away and the runt with the half-brick threatened again. (How I wished at the moment we could meet man to man.) Someone yelled: 'Don't kill him.' It was repeated by another in the mob as I staggered toward my car. Someone gave me a punch from the rear, adding to the impetus of my retreat.

"Suddenly, I was free of the pack. One man yelled, 'We'll teach you northern niggers about coming down here.' What the bigoted creature didn't know is that I am one of many southern-born citizens dedicated to the cause of helping bring full democracy to this great country of ours."

While the mob was attacking Alex Wilson and the other black newsmen, the Little Rock Nine slipped quickly into the side entrance of the school, escorted by the police. The students entered easily because the mob was focused on the black newsmen, but once word got out that the students were in the school, the mob left the black adults. As one of the black newsmen told Mrs. Bates, "We probably saved you and the children, but I know you saved us....when they [the mob] charged toward the school we got the hell out of there."

Policemen stood in front of sawhorse barricades, trying to hold back the mob, which was estimated at 300 at the time the newsmen arrived and grew steadily until there were more than a thousand by noon. Reporters who checked car license plates in the area

determined that many of them were from other counties, although there were plenty of local people, too. Governor Faubus's friend Jimmy Karam was in the streets. Mayor Mann believed he played a role in organizing the mob, but this has never been proven.

According to a local newspaper account, "The crowd roamed through the streets, trying repeatedly to break through the police line and get into the School. Husky men and boys fought with the police, newsmen and bypassing Negroes, broke out car windows, and once tried to tip over a pickup truck containing two Negro men. Women and teenage girls stood sobbing and pleading with white students to leave the School, and some parents went into the School to retrieve their children from the classrooms."

Among the sobbing women was Mary Thomason, who had sued the school board to try to stop integration. She screamed at the men around her, "Where's your manhood? Why don't you do something to get these people?" Then she broke down in tears, wailing, "My daughter's in there with those niggers. Oh, my God! Oh, God!"

Inside the school, the scene was calmer, but there was still name-calling, staring, threats, and nasty incidents. The nine students went to the office first, where Thelma Mothershed, who had a heart condition, slumped down on a wooden bench, gasping for breath and with her heart beating irregularly. The school nurse stayed with her while the other eight students were escorted to their first classes by members of the school staff.

Mary Thomason

Melba Pattillo remembered feeling "alone, in a daze" as she followed a stocky white woman up the stairs toward her third-floor classroom. "I had fantasized about how wonderful it would be to get inside the huge beautiful castle I knew as Central High School. But the reality was so much bigger, darker and more treacherous than I had imagined. I could easily get lost among its spiral staircases. The angry voices shouting at me made it...more difficult to find my way through these unfamiliar surroundings."

Falling behind her guide, Melba felt "the sting of a hand slapping my cheek, and then warm slimy saliva on my face dropping to the collar of my blouse." She found herself standing face-to-face with a middle-age white woman, probably the mother of a student who had come to take her child out of school.

"'Nigger!' she shouted in my face again and again....Her face was distorted by rage. 'Nigger bitch! Why don't you go home?' she lashed out at me. 'Next thing, you'll want to marry one of our children!'"

Wiping the spit from her face, Melba moved quickly around the woman and caught up to her guide. In the classroom the teacher ignored her, and when she took a seat, the students around her picked up their books and moved away. "Are you gonna let that nigger coon sit in our class?" a boy asked. The teacher made no response, but tried to continue her lesson, only to be interrupted by the same boy. "We can kick the crap out of this nigger....It's twenty of us and one of her. They ain't nothing but animals."

Not all classroom experiences were as bad as Melba's, and not all white students acted like the boy in her first class. A white junior named Robin Woods later told a reporter: "If there was trouble at Central High yesterday, it was all on the outside. We didn't have anything at all going on inside. I got integrated yesterday. It was in my first English class. There was only 15 minutes to go, and a Negro boy [Terrence Roberts] came into class. That was the first time I'd ever gone to school with a Negro, and it didn't hurt a bit."

Five years later in a 1962 television interview, Ernest Green recalled: "...of all the things that have happened at Central, the most significant thing was the friendly attitude that students showed toward me the day of the rioting.

"The type of thing that was going on outside, people beaten, cursed, the mob hysterics and all of this going on outside...we inside the school didn't realize the

Robin Woods

35

Charles Oakley

problems that were occurring and continually students were befriending us. I remember one case in particular in my physics class. I was three weeks behind in my assignments, and a couple of fellows offered to give me notes and to help me catch up the work that I had missed. I was amazed at this kind of attitude being shown toward the Negroes."

The "couple of fellows" were Charles Oakley and Steve Swafford. Fifty years later, Charles was asked why he helped Ernest that first day: "Well, why not? He's coming into class three weeks late and he doesn't have this stuff [notes]....Ernest had not been exposed to white students who wanted to say, 'Welcome. This is a tough school....Good luck.'"

Shortly before noon, Assistant Police Chief Gene Smith, who was in charge of law enforcement on the scene, decided that it would be safer to get the black students out

Ernest Green discusses a physics experiment with fellow senior Harper Thomason. Physics class, which included many of the top seniors at Central, was a safe haven where Ernest experienced a friendly, helpful attitude from several white students.

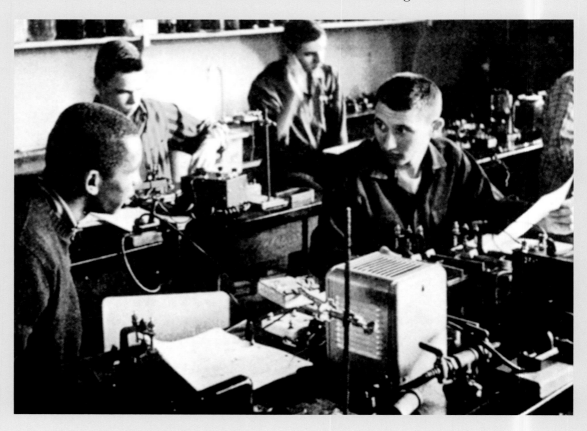

before the end of classes. The mob had grown so large and violent that he feared his men could no longer keep them back. Many white policemen were more sympathetic to the mob than to the black students. At least one took off his badge and resigned on the spot, and there were rumors of others joining the mob. It is still said in Little Rock that Gene Smith—a big strong man—saved the students that day because the Little Rock policemen were more afraid of Smith than they were of the mob.

On Smith's orders, the nine black students were taken out of their classes and led down into a basement garage, where two police cars were waiting for them. "Put your foot to the floor," Smith told the drivers, "and don't stop for anyone!" As the garage door opened, the cars sped out across a gravel driveway and into the street. Melba Pattillo remembered someone shouting, "Hang those niggers! Stop those cars!" and seeing "wave after wave of white faces, angry white faces, everywhere." The cars broke through the mob and took the children safely home. "Had the mob been a little quicker," Terrence Roberts said, "we might have all been killed. We got out just in time."

Jefferson Thomas remembered, "My mother was on the front porch crying when we pulled up, and I couldn't understand why she was so upset. Then we went into the house and turned the television on." Together, they watched footage of the mob beating the black newsmen as the students entered the school. That was the first time Jefferson realized how close they had come to being beaten themselves. "That's what protected us—the news personnel trying to get a story."

Little Rock Police Officer Tommy Dunaway—a graduate of Central High—chooses to resign from the force rather than use his billy club against Little Rock citizens who protested on September 23. A collection taken up for him that morning raised about $105.

Jefferson Thomas

Paratroopers from the 101st Airborne Division run down the middle of Park Street, the road facing the main entrance to Central High, on the morning of September 25, 1957. Their orders were to get the Little Rock Nine safely into the school.

september 25, 1957

From his vacation home in Newport, Rhode Island, President Eisenhower closely followed the events in Little Rock. In the early afternoon of September 23, while the mob still roamed outside Central High, he issued a statement saying, "I will use the full power of the United States including whatever force may be necessary to prevent any obstruction of the law and to carry out the orders of the federal court." Eisenhower had made clear in previous statements that he did not want to use federal troops to enforce integration, but now he referred to laws that gave the president the power to do exactly that if the mob in Little Rock did not "cease and desist...[and] disperse."

The Little Rock Nine stayed home the following day, but Ernest Green confirmed to a reporter that they were not giving up. "My first day inside Central High was very smooth—smoother than I expected....If it wasn't for the people outside, we would have finished the day. But I don't intend to quit. We'll try again. It's still my school, and I'm entitled to it."

On the morning of September 24, a mob of about 400 gathered outside the school. Since the black students did not arrive, many of the protesters began to leave, and the police seemed to be in control of the situation. However, Mayor Mann and other city leaders had already decided to send a telegram to President Eisenhower asking him to send federal troops. In wording the telegram, they worked with government lawyers under U.S. Attorney General Herbert Brownell, who believed that sending federal troops would send a message to other states that were resisting integration.

"The immediate need for federal troops is urgent," the mayor's telegram began. "...Mob is armed and engaging in fisticuffs and other acts of violence. Situation is out of control...I am pleading to you as President of the United States in the interest of humanity law and order and because of democracy world wide to provide the necessary federal troops within several hours."

The telegram was sent at 9:16 a.m., and a little more than two hours later, President Eisenhower ordered the 101st Airborne Division to leave their base in

Ernest Green

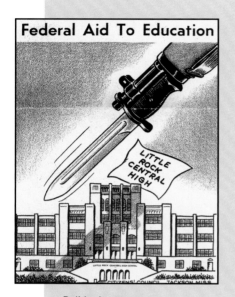

Federal Aid To Education

Political cartoons about the Little Rock crisis appeared in newspapers around the world. This one from the *Citizens' Council* of Jackson, Mississippi, vividly protests the use of federal military force to integrate Central High School.

Daisy Bates

Kentucky and fly to Little Rock. Known as the Screaming Eagles, the 101st was among the most famous and honored Army divisions for its heroism in World War II and the Korean War. A force of 856 soldiers landed in Little Rock that afternoon. By that evening, more than 300 surrounded Central High under the command of General Edwin Walker. Almost 100 more arrived the next day, and 500 others waited in Kentucky to be used as needed.

When not on duty at the school, the soldiers stayed at Camp Robinson outside of Little Rock. After the first day, all black soldiers stayed in reserve at Camp Robinson because the Army believed that the presence of black soldiers would inflame the mob.

The President's order also federalized the Arkansas National Guard. This meant that Governor Faubus was no longer their commander-in-chief. Instead they would be under the command of General Walker.

That evening, President Eisenhower, now back in the White House, addressed the American people on radio and television, explaining his action in the Little Rock crisis. "Mob rule cannot be allowed to override the decisions of our courts," he said. "...The overwhelming majority of our people in every section of the country are united in their respect for observance of the law—even in those cases where they may disagree with that law....A foundation of our American way of life is our national respect for law."

On the morning of Wednesday, September 25—just two days after the rioting—the Little Rock Nine once again gathered at the home of Daisy and L.C. Bates. Around 9 a.m., a convoy of Army vehicles arrived. Two jeeps carrying combat-ready paratroopers passed the Bates's home and stopped at one end of the street, and two other jeeps stopped at the opposite end. The paratroopers jumped out and guarded each end of the street while an Army station wagon pulled to the curb outside the Bates's house. An officer came to the door and saluted. "Mrs. Bates," he said, "we're ready for the children. We will return them to your home at three thirty o'clock."

"The streets were blocked off," Daisy Bates recalled. "The soldiers closed ranks. Neighbors came out and looked. The street was full up and down. Oh, it was beautiful. And the attitude of the children at that moment, the respect they had. I could hear

Carlotta Walls (left) and Minnijean Brown hurry out of an Army station wagon during the first days of integration at Central High. On October 1 federalized Arkansas National Guard under General Edwin Walker replaced the 101st Airborne. There was trouble immediately, and the 101st returned two days later, sharing peacekeeping duties with the federalized National Guard until Thanksgiving.

them saying, 'For the first time in my life I truly feel like an American.' I could see it in their faces; somebody cares for me, America cares."

With tears in her eyes—and photographers hanging off her roof to capture the moment—Mrs. Bates and the parents watched the nine students climb into the Army station wagon. Minnijean Brown remembered that one of the soldiers called her "Ma'am" as he held the door for her. "We'd never been treated like that...by anyone, and certainly not by any white people. That was the first time we actually felt free to be ourselves, and we were just giggling and making jokes. It was a really good feeling." With one jeep in front of the station wagon, another behind, and a police car bringing up the rear with siren blaring, the convoy headed for Central High, less than two miles away.

At the school, 350 stern-faced soldiers armed with rifles and bayonets had sealed off the area, allowing only students and reporters through their lines. Spectators who didn't move were dealt with quickly. Two white female students who wanted to watch instead of going on to school were marched on their way with sharp bayonets at their backs. A photo shows them laughing as they walked, as if it were all a joke. Two white men who resisted discovered that the soldiers were deadly serious. One was stabbed in his arm by a bayonet and the other was smashed across his face with a rifle butt.

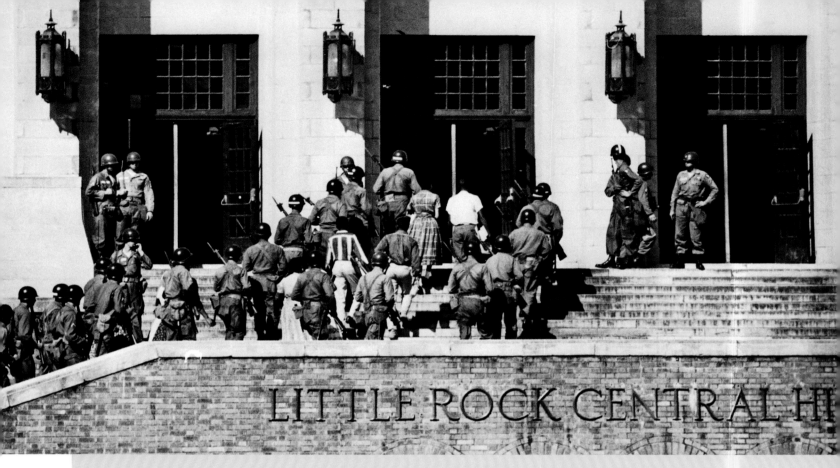

LITTLE ROCK CENTRAL HI

Escorted by troops of the 101st Airborne, the Little Rock Nine enter Central High through the front doors on the morning of September 25, 1957. This historic moment is celebrated as the anniversary of integration at Central High and as one of the greatest moments of America's Civil Rights Movement.

When the Army convoy arrived from the Bates's house, the area outside the school was almost silent except for the siren of the police car and the drone of an Army helicopter flying overhead. The station wagon pulled up outside the main entrance of the school, where Elizabeth Eckford had been denied entrance by the Arkansas National Guard exactly three weeks earlier. The nine students emerged from the car and were escorted by 22 paratroopers down a long sidewalk and up three sets of stairs to the majestic front entrance of Central High.

"I felt very special at that moment," remembered Terrence Roberts. "I was aware that something momentous was taking place that morning although years would pass before I would truly grasp the overall significance of what had happened. This was the first time since Reconstruction that federal troops had been ordered into the South to protect the rights of African Americans. On that morning, however, my primary thought was that maybe now I would not be killed for simply trying to go to school."

There was a crowd of white students outside the entrance, forming a sort of barricade, and Elizabeth Eckford remembered that they moved aside for the soldiers. "That was a triumphant moment for me...like parting the Red Sea. The students were chanting, 'Two, four, six, eight, we don't want to integrate,' and we developed this line to ourselves: 'Eight, nine, ten, the guards will take us in.'"

At 9:22 a.m. the Little Rock Nine walked through the tall wooden doors. An Army photographer snapped a photograph from the inside as they entered, and Principal Jess Matthews greeted them as if it were any other day, saying, "Well, good morning, boys and girls; this is the first class period, and you all know your way to that class." The students continued in different directions, each with a soldier following behind. The soldiers did not enter any of the classrooms, but waited outside the door until it was time for their student to go to the next class.

Just before the black students arrived, General Walker had spoken to the white students in an all-school assembly. "You have nothing to fear from my soldiers," he said, "and no one will interfere with your coming, going, or your peaceful pursuit of your studies….However, I would be less than honest if I failed to tell you that I intend to use all means necessary to prevent any interference with your school board's plan. This is what I have been ordered to do, and I intend to carry out my orders. Those who interfere or disrupt the proper administration of the school will be removed by the soldiers on duty and turned over to the local police for disposition in accordance with the laws of your community."

The general's no-nonsense military message made a powerful impression on the students who heard him. "He got up in front of the student body," remembered senior Lee Johnson, "and he pretty well laid the law down. He let it be known they weren't going to tolerate any kind of trouble."

Unfortunately, many of the students who really needed to hear the general's message—the dedicated segregationists—were absent that day, and more left after the assembly. In Arkansas at that time, students were not required to go to high school, so they could leave or stay home at any time.

Elizabeth Huckaby, an English teacher and vice principal for girls, remembered that, right after the assembly, "Most of the students went on to class. Some lingered uncertainly or belligerently in the corridor. 'If you're not staying in school, go sign out,' we told them.' About eighty signed out."

General Edwin Walker

Railroad worker C.E. Blake of North Little Rock stands stunned and bleeding after being clubbed by rifle butts when he resisted orders from the 101st Airborne.

Elizabeth Huckaby

Hundreds more had already decided to stay home. Out of almost 2,000 enrolled students, approximately 750 were absent on September 25.

Other students continued to leave throughout the day. "Every class I walked into," Terrence Roberts recalled, "a contingent of students got up and left. They gave me the benefit of their best thinking about me and people like me, and they said, 'We're not coming back as long as you're here.'"

A white student named Jerry Butler, who saw the sign-out book, remembered, "There were just pages and pages in that book of people who had written their name, and, at the side, where they wrote the reason to leave, they had written 'coon' and 'nigger' and all kinds of racial statements."

Except for the walkouts, the white students were quiet inside the school, but the segregationists continued to work from outside. At 11:30 a.m. Principal Matthews received an anonymous call telling him that the school would be blown up at noon. All students were evacuated onto the broad front lawn facing Park Street, where reporters and photographers—who were not allowed inside the school—eagerly shouted questions and snapped photos of black and white students standing together and talking. Although typical fire drills lasted three minutes, it took a half hour for a demolition team to check lockers, classrooms, and other areas for bombs. This was the first of at least 43 bomb threats that would disrupt school throughout the year.

The huge cafeteria at Central would later become a battleground, but on that first full day of integration it was peaceful. The school was so large that there were two different lunch periods. During the first period, a group of five white students—four girls and one boy—invited the black students who had lunch that period to sit with them.

Glennys Oakes

One of the white girls, a pretty, smart senior named Glennys Oakes, recalled, "There was a group of us who were all involved in the Senior High Fellowship at our church, and we sat together at lunch. We had talked about integration during our fellowship meetings that summer, and our minister explained to us that the Biblical argument for segregation came from the story of Noah. One of his sons was supposed to be dark-skinned and he was cast out. We all read that passage [Genesis: 9:20–27], and our minister thought this was a ridiculous interpretation, and so did I. Our whole perspective was that this [integration] was the right thing to do." Glennys maintained

Minnijean Brown laughs with fellow students during a bomb threat evacuation on September 25, the first full day of integration. In a recent interview, Minnijean said of this photo, "At that time, I still thought we could all be friends." It didn't work out that way.

the "open table" policy all year and was often harassed for it by the segregationists. Sometime before Christmas, she found a big, white cross—a symbol of the Ku Klux Klan—planted on her lawn.

When the school day was over, the nine black students again were escorted by soldiers to the Army station wagon and returned to the Bates's home by 3:30 p.m., just as the officer had promised. There they shared their experiences of the day and were interviewed by a small group of reporters before moving on to the community center for a more formal press conference. Most of the students were cautious in their statements, but Melba Pattillo and Minnijean Brown, the two most vivacious and outspoken of the Little Rock Nine, expressed a real sense of excitement about their first full day at school.

"I had a good time," said Melba. "The only incidents were very, very minor....When I walked into one class a boy got up and made a speech, urging the other students to walk out. He told the others that they were 'chicken' if they didn't walk out. Then the teacher told him to leave and he left. Everybody else stayed."

"Today was a very exciting day," answered Minnijean. When asked what the white students thought of her, she gave an interesting and thoughtful reply: "They are anxious to find out what we are like. They are torn between their parents and their own minds. They just don't know what to do."

On this she was absolutely right. This experience was new for all the students, black and white. In the weeks and months that followed, every student at Central High would have to make difficult decisions.

After a day of classes, Thelma Mothershed (left) and Melba Pattillo leave Central High and enter an Army station wagon under heavy guard by soldiers of the 101st Airborne. The Army escort ended on Friday, October 25. From that day until the end of the year, the Nine came to school in carpools arranged by their parents.

student warriors

September 25, 1957, is celebrated as the day that Central High was integrated. It is among the most significant civil rights anniversaries in the United States, but for the Little Rock Nine it was only the beginning of a long, painful year.

The 101st Airborne kept the mob of protesters away from the school, but the segregationists did not give up. They continued to fight integration at Central High through bomb threats and a campaign of threatening phone calls to the families of the Little Rock Nine and anyone who helped them. They pressured employers to fire parents of the Nine and boycotted businesses that advertised in the *State Press,* published by L.C. and Daisy Bates, and in the *Arkansas Gazette,* a white newspaper that supported integration.

Adult segregationists worked with like-minded students to organize harassment of the Little Rock Nine in school, and there were plenty of other high school troublemakers who didn't need organization to abuse the black newcomers. Estimates of the number of students who actively harassed the Nine range from 50 to 200. Whatever the number, there were more than enough to make life miserable for them.

Day after day, the Nine faced insults, threats, and physical violence. They endured punching, shoving, and kicking. They had spitballs, rubber bands, and paper clips shot at them, their heels stepped on by white students walking behind them, ink sprayed on their clothes, knives flashed in their faces, and their heads and clothing shoved into toilets. Glue and tacks and glass were placed on their seats, and their gym showers were turned to scalding hot. Their lockers were broken into and their books were stolen or destroyed so often that many of them stopped carrying books to school. These were everyday events. Some days were worse than others.

Elizabeth Eckford and Gloria Ray were pushed down the stairs in two separate incidents. Melba Pattillo had acid thrown in her eyes and her sight was saved only by the quick action of her 101st Airborne guard who rinsed it out repeatedly with water. Terrence Roberts had a gym lock thrown at his head, opening a gash. Jefferson

This cartoon by a Central High student suggests that the Nine were under so much protection that they might as well have been wearing armor.

Two Central High students wearing symbols of the Confederacy talk with a reporter outside the school on October 3, the day of the organized walkout.

Jim Eison

Thomas was knocked unconscious by a blow from behind while standing at his locker. The list goes on and on.

For about a week the Nine had personal guards from the 101st Airborne, but the guards only followed them in the hallways, a number of steps behind. They did not go into the classrooms, restrooms, locker rooms, or the cafeteria. And even in the halls, there were limits on what they could do. On the second full day of integration, Melba was knocked down on her way to homeroom class by a group of boys.

"One of them kicked me in the shins so hard I fell to the floor," she wrote. "A second kick was delivered to my stomach. [My guard] stood over me, motioning them to move away....I struggled to my feet. More white students gathered around and taunted me, applauding and cheering: 'The nigger's down.'"

When Melba asked her guard why he didn't stop the boys immediately, he explained, "I'm here for one thing. To keep you alive. I'm not allowed to get into verbal or physical battles with these students."

On Thursday, October 3, a group of white students—organized by the Mothers League—staged a walkout to protest the presence of the black students in their school. Although approximately 150 left, about half circled back and reentered the school when they realized that fewer students walked out than expected. The rest crossed Park Street to a vacant lot at the corner of 16th Street.

There they hung a straw-filled dummy of a black student from a big oak tree, near where Elizabeth had sat on the bench on September 4. They danced around it, kicking it, punching it, stabbing it, and setting it on fire. As one boy stabbed the effigy with a penknife, a photographer at the scene asked another boy standing nearby what he was thinking. "Oh, if that were only a real one!" he said.

The boy who said it, Jim Eison, grew up to be a historian for two Little Rock museums. Forty years later, at a time when there were many public apologies for the events at Central, he offered an unusual but honest perspective: "I was a product of my day and time, and I was acting from my early upbringing....The sentiment was true.

I'd rather I hadn't said it, but at the same time I'm stubborn enough that I don't like people to make statements and then apologize....I want to caution people against judging people of the past, unless they were here and understood the situation."

Shortly after the walkout, Sammie Dean Parker and Kay Bacon, two of the girls who had worked with the Mothers League to organize it, participated in a panel discussion with Ernest Green, Minnijean Brown, Melba Pattillo, and two "moderate" white students: Joe Fox and Robin Woods. The discussion, which had been organized by Robin at the request of a foreign journalist, was held on a Saturday afternoon and later broadcast on NBC radio.

Sammie Dean, when asked if she thought it was possible to work out the problems at Central without more violence, replied: "No, I don't, because the South has always been against racial mixing and I think they will fight this thing to the end....We fight for our freedom—that's one thing. And we don't have any freedom anymore."

Ernest Green pointed out, "If anybody should kick about freedoms, it should be us." Joe Fox said, "Well, Sammie, I don't know what freedom has been taken away from you. The troops haven't kept me from going to my classes or participating in any school activity."

Minnijean tried to make the white girls understand that she was very much like them. "Hold your hand up," she said to Sammie Dean. "I'm brown; you're white. What's the difference? We are all of the same thoughts. You're thinking about your boy[friend]—he's going to the Navy. I'm thinking about mine—he's in the Air Force. We think about the same thing."

By the end of the discussion, Kay and Sammie claimed they had changed their minds. "We both came down here today with our mind set," Kay explained. "But I know now that we're going to change our mind....I'm going to have a long talk with my parents."

During the walkout, a student stabs a straw dummy of a black student hanging from a tree across from Central High. The effigy was designed as a prank by a couple of seniors who planned to hang it out of a school window before they "chickened out." Other students found it in a school bathroom and carried it across the street.

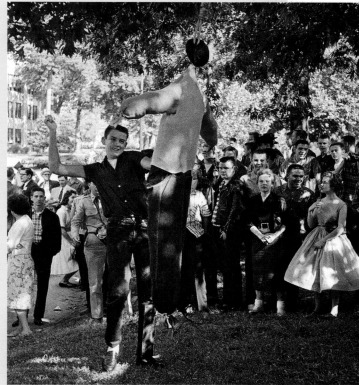

Whether Kay really changed her mind is not clear. Sammie Dean's actions show that she did not. As the year progressed she became the most visible and vocal leader of the segregationist students, as well as a connection between segregationist adults outside the school and the students inside.

Dealing with hostile students was only one of the challenges faced by the Nine. They also had to deal with hostile teachers. Terrence Roberts remembered that his English teacher "was so terribly unwelcoming. She said to me one day, 'Why do you want to come to our school? Why don't you go back to your own school?'"

Thelma Mothershed recalled that her homeroom teacher "did strange little things....[W]hen we were absent, we'd have to go to the office and get a readmittance slip. When I would come in to give her my readmittance slip, she wouldn't take it. So I would just put it down on the desk, and then she would sign it and put it in the book and slide it back across to me....So she did little strange, subtle things—subtle as a ton of bricks." The not-so subtle message was that the teacher would not touch a piece of paper at the same time a black student touched it.

Below are the seven students who participated in the panel discussion for NBC radio. In front are Sammie Dean Parker (left) and Robin Woods. Behind them are Kay Bacon, Melba Pattillo, and Minnijean Brown. In the back are Ernest Green and Joe Fox.

Other teachers made the black students welcome. "Algebra class was a haven for me," Terrence Roberts wrote. "The teacher, Mrs. Helen Conrad, let it be known from the first day that I was in class that she would not tolerate any nonsense from anyone who opposed my presence. She was emphatic about it and the class responded accordingly."

Some white students tried to show friendship, or at least politeness, to the newcomers. But most were quickly intimidated by the segregationists. "They isolated them," Ernest Green explained, "and intimidated or threatened their family businesses, called them up in the middle of the night,...called them nigger lovers." Despite this intimidation, a handful of white students maintained their friendly relations with the blacks.

Elizabeth Eckford, Jefferson Thomas, and Terrence Roberts (with back to camera) eat lunch in the Central High cafeteria, which would become the scene of several conflicts involving Minnijean Brown and some white students.

Robin Woods was labeled a nigger lover and chased home the day she shared her algebra book with Terrence Roberts after his book was stolen. But she refused to be intimidated and continued to share her book and show friendship to him throughout the year. She received threatening letters and phone calls, had rocks thrown at her, and was spit upon by segregtionists.

"Melba Pattillo and I walked down the halls at times together," recalled Margaret Johnson. "If we went the same way more than once, there were students who would be taunting. I could handle name-calling, but to this day, I am afraid of being pushed and shoved both up and down stairs and always use the wall side of a set of stairs."

Ann Williams and Ken Reinhardt befriended Elizabeth Eckford in speech class. "The first day, she was sitting by herself away from everyone else," Ann recalled. "I realized how lonely she must have felt and what courage it took to be there. I went over and sat by her. We were often speech partners and became life-long friends." Ann lived on a farm outside the city, and her father had to hire armed guards to protect their home. Ken was continually harassed in gym class, knocked down many times, and punched in the face on the last day of school...all with no action by the teacher.

Not all students who helped the Nine suffered for their actions. Charles Oakley and Steve Swafford continued to work with Ernest Green as physics lab partners throughout the year. They were seniors, athletes on the track team, and physics was not the kind of class that the troublemakers took. "Charlie and I never really discussed our actions," Steve recalled, "but it was just understood that we would attempt, whenever possible, to help Ernest assemble the experimental apparatus....Tests were a different matter. Then it was every man for himself. We all passed."

Margaret Johnson

Steve Swafford

Ralph Brodie

Justlyn Matlock

Between the extremes of the troublemakers and the students who actively helped the Little Rock Nine were the "silent majority," who went about the daily business of getting an education. The actions of this silent majority still cause controversy today. Elizabeth Eckford speaks of "silent witnesses" who watched harm being done but did nothing to stop it. Ralph Brodie, student body president that year, says, "Like most of my senior classmates, I never saw a single act of hostility. I heard rumors that some students were harassing the black students, and I went to the principal several times to ask if I or the student council could help with the situation, but each time I was told that the problem was under control."

Justlyn Matlock, a senior that year, explains, "Many of us had no animosity and wanted to help make the situation better for everyone, but we didn't know how. We decided that any attempt to intervene had the potential for causing more harm. So, we went about our role as students and left the confrontation with anger and chaos to the professional forces."

The professional forces changed after Thanksgiving, when the 101st Airborne returned to their base in Kentucky and were replaced by the federalized Arkansas National Guard under the command of General Walker. This was a move to calm the anger of white Southerners over what they saw as federal "occupation," but it increased the personal danger of the Little Rock Nine. The Guardsmen were very young, many just out of high school, and they did not have the training of the professional soldiers. They also did not have the same commitment to enforcing federal law. Many were the same soldiers who had originally kept the Nine out of Central. Harassment inside Central reached new levels in December.

Before school began, the Nine had agreed to face their struggle without fighting back. However, sometimes it was just too much to bear.

On December 17 Minnijean Brown walked toward the lunch table where she usually sat, carrying a tray with a bowl of hot chili. She found her path blocked by a fellow junior named Dent Gitchel. As Dent later explained, he was not trying to block her. The aisle was very narrow, and he was trying to push his chair in so Minnijean could pass. "The boy sitting facing me placed his feet on the front legs of my chair so that I could not move. That's the last thing I remember before I felt a bump on the head."

The "bump on the head" was Minnijean's tray with the hot chili, which spilled on Dent and another boy sitting nearby. "I had no thoughts at that moment,"

Minnijean said in a recent interview. "I just opened my hands and let the tray drop."

"Pandemonium broke loose," Dent recalled. "There were hundreds of kids in the lunch room and everybody's on their seats screaming and hollering." Ernest Green remembered that the all-black kitchen help broke into applause for Minnijean.

The two boys went to the principal's office followed a short time later by Minnijean, who admitted that she had dropped her tray "accidentally on purpose." Dent Gitchel, his shirt stained with chili, defended her. Dent doesn't remember what he said that day, but both Minnijean and Vice Principal Huckaby remembered him expressing sympathy for the abuse that Minnijean had faced.

Despite Dent's sympathetic attitude, Principal Matthews suspended Minnijean. After the Christmas holidays she returned on probation, meaning she would be expelled if she was involved in another incident. She was switched to another lunch period, where she, along with some other members of the Nine, shared a table with Glennys Oakes and several other white students. In mid-January a boy dumped hot soup on her head while she was sitting at the table.

"The lunch room erupted," Glennys remembered. "Kids all around us were clamoring up on top of the tables, yelling and screaming, raising their arms and stomping their feet to cheer. I was acutely aware that I, my friends, and those black students were at the center of a near riot....These were students that I saw every day, was acquainted with many of them, and yet on that day, they were a mob."

The attacks on Minnijean continued until the morning of February 6 when a white girl named Frankie Gregg—who had been harassing Minnijean all week—threw a purse at her and hit her in the back of the head. Minnijean picked up the purse and

On September 27—the third full day of integration—Gloria Ray waits her turn to bat during girls' gym class. In another part of the athletic field, laundry hangs from Army vehicles, and members of the 101st take a break from guard duty.

Dent Gitchel

53

Minnijean Brown says goodbye to Ernest Green and the rest of the Little Rock Nine after her expulsion from Central High in February 1958.

Gloria Ray found this card on her assigned desk in one of her classrooms after Minnijean left.

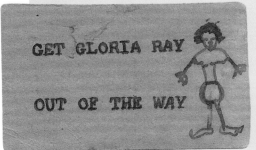

GET GLORIA RAY OUT OF THE WAY

discovered that it was full of combination locks to make it heavier. Instead of throwing it back she dropped it at her feet, saying, "Leave me alone, white trash."

That afternoon, after Minnijean was "souped" again at lunch, Principal Matthews suspended her again—not for being souped but because her "white trash" remark violated her probation. Eleven days later the school board expelled her from all Little Rock schools for the rest of the year. In her memoir, Vice Principal Huckaby admitted that the situation was simply out of control. "The truth, of course, was that we could no longer run the school if Minnijean was there."

"I just can't take everything they throw at me without fighting back," Minnijean told a reporter at the time. "I don't think people realize what goes on at Central. You just wouldn't believe it. They throw rocks, they spill ink on your clothes, they call you 'nigger,' they just keep bothering you every five minutes. The white students hate me. Why do they hate me so much?"

Minnijean went to New York City, where she attended a private high school. Although she finished school in a better environment, she felt that she had let the rest of the Nine down. But her fellow black students never blamed her for fighting back. "We were proud of Minnijean for doing what we all wanted to do so badly," wrote Terrence Roberts. "She had acted as our proxy in giving back a small measure of what we had to endure."

Minnijean's departure was a triumph for the segregationist students, who passed out cards that read, "ONE DOWN...EIGHT TO GO." Daily harassment became even worse, but the Eight refused to give in. "They don't want me in the school. They want me to quit," recalled Jefferson Thomas. "As long as I don't quit, I'm a winner."

Gloria Ray remembered the pain of the daily torment. "For me, walking in the hallways of Central that year, especially after Minnijean's departure, was like walking in Hell! In the school we didn't meet each other....I didn't share one class with another black person." Somehow, with courage and maturity beyond their years—and the support of their loving families—the eight remaining black students made it through that horrible year.

As graduation approached, harassment of Ernest Green, the only senior in the group, increased—with threats, phone calls, and other pressure on him to stay away from the graduation ceremony. In an anonymous letter, "a worried senior" wrote: "Naturally you deserve your sheepskin [diploma] as much as anyone, and I would not stop you from getting it. However, there are, as you well know, many who would gladly do so. Therefore, I am asking you Earnest [sic] to please refrain from attending these exercises. It will be a time that I and hundreds of others do not wish to have marred."

Despite the threats and pressure, Ernest was determined to finish what he had started. "There was no way I wasn't going to show up for the ceremony."

The graduation ceremony was held on the evening of Tuesday, May 27, in the football stadium. Although there were plenty of policemen, the National Guard stayed out of sight. General Walker had stationed two fully armed, combat-ready platoons under the bleachers where they could not be seen. The atmosphere was tense, and the tension grew as the names of graduates were read and the time approached for the first black graduate of Central High to receive his diploma.

Ernest Green receives his diploma from Principal Jess Matthews. Later, at Daisy Bates's house, he was congratulated on his achievement by the Reverend Martin Luther King, Jr.

"There were a lot of claps for the [white] students," Ernest recalled. "They talked about who had received scholarships, who was an honor student, and all that as they called the names off. When they called my name there was nothing, just the name, and there was this eerie silence. Nobody clapped. But I figured they didn't have to. Because after I got that diploma, that was it. I had accomplished what I had come there for."

Although Ernest didn't know until later that evening, Dr. Martin Luther King, Jr., was in the stadium, watching him accept his "sheepskin." What Ernest and the rest of the Little Rock Nine did was not only for themselves but also for the same dream that Dr. King preached and later died for—the dream of a better America, where freedom and opportunity do not depend on the color of your skin.

In "Testament," a life-size sculpture by artists John and Kathy Deering,
the Little Rock Nine are honored in bronze on the grounds of the Arkansas State Capitol,
not far from where they made history at Central High School.

epilogue

During the summer of 1958, the Little Rock Nine, along with Daisy Bates, received several awards for their courageous effort, including the NAACP's prestigious Spingarn Medal, honoring the highest achievement by black Americans. Meanwhile, the integration crisis continued to divide Little Rock.

On August 28 the state legislature passed a series of anti-integration laws, including one that allowed Governor Faubus to close the public schools and call a special election on the issue. On September 12 the U.S. Supreme Court ruled that integration must proceed, and Faubus closed all four public high schools in Little Rock. Fifteen days later, the people of Little Rock rejected integration by a vote of 19,470 to 7,561. At this time, many believed—wrongly—that integration could be avoided by leasing the public schools to a private corporation.

The high schools remained closed for the entire 1958–59 school year. About 1,050 white students attended two new private high schools, while about 2,500 others, black and white, had to find alternate ways to continue their education. Some did not go to school at all.

With the high schools closed, the moderate citizens of Little Rock, led by a group of white women called the Women's Emergency Committee, spoke out in favor of obeying federal law. A key turning point came in March 1959 when the Little Rock Chamber of Commerce, realizing that the crisis was damaging business in the city, voted to accept integrated schools.

By this time the original school board had resigned, and the new six-member board was evenly split between moderates and segregationists. In May 1958 the segregationists attempted to fire 44 teachers and administrators suspected of pro-integration sympathies, but the moderates refused to participate in the vote. In a special election on May 25 the citizens of Little Rock "recalled" (removed) the three segregationist members, who were later replaced by moderates.

The high schools reopened on August 12, 1959. Jefferson Thomas and another black student returned to Central that day, later joined by Carlotta Walls. Three black girls attended Hall High. Segregationists rallied at the state capitol and marched toward Central, carrying American flags and protest signs. The Little Rock police arrested 21 troublemakers, and Police Chief Gene Smith ordered fire hoses turned on those who tried to cross the police line in front of Central High.

Integration progressed slowly, working downward from the high schools, and it was not until 1972 that all Little Rock public schools were integrated. Today, Central High is an award-winning school where students of all races and ethnic backgrounds can participate together in the educational experience.

TIME LINE OF THE CIVIL RIGHTS MOVEMENT

Civil rights are basic rights and privileges guaranteed to all citizens by the U.S. Constitution, its amendments, and other laws. At the time the Constitution and the first ten Amendments, called the Bill of Rights, became law (1789 and 1791), most black Americans were slaves and considered property rather than citizens. This changed with the Emancipation Proclamation of 1863, the passage of the 13th, 14th, and 15th Amendments (1865–1870), and the Civil Rights Act of 1866. These laws abolished slavery and granted citizenship and basic human rights to everyone born in America, regardless of race or color (except American Indians).

After Reconstruction (1865–1877) former Confederate states and a number of others passed so-called Jim Crow laws, which limited the rights of black citizens and legalized segregation (separation) of the races. In 1896 the U.S. Supreme Court ruled in *Plessy v. Ferguson* that segregation was legal so long as there were "separate but equal" facilities for whites and blacks.

The Civil Rights Movement is the battle of black Americans to overturn the concept of "separate but equal" and claim their full rights as American citizens. This time line includes some of the key events in that battle—a battle that has won more rights for all Americans, regardless of race, color, religion, national origin, gender, age, or disability.

Dec. 18, 1865 The 13th Amendment abolishes slavery in the U.S.

Dec. 24, 1865 The Ku Klux Klan, a white supremacist organization, is formed in Tennessee.

1865–1867 All former slave states pass Black Codes, restricting the rights of former slaves.

Apr. 9, 1866 The Civil Rights Act of 1866 grants citizenship to all individuals born in the United States—except Indians.

July 9, 1868 The 14th Amendment guarantees all citizens due process and equal protection of the law.

Feb. 3, 1870 The 15th Amendment guarantees all male citizens the right to vote, regardless of race, color, or previous servitude.

Mar. 1, 1875 The Civil Rights Act of 1875 guarantees equal access to inns, transportation, theaters, and other public places to all citizens.

Oct. 16, 1883 The U.S. Supreme Court declares the Civil Rights Act of 1875 unconstitutional. This ruling opens the door for the states to pass new segregation laws called Jim Crow laws.

May 18, 1896 In *Plessy v. Ferguson* the U.S. Supreme Court rules that "separate but equal facilities" are legal.

May 1909 The National Association for the Advancement of Colored People (NAACP) holds its first national conference.

1913–14 President Woodrow Wilson permits segregation of federal facilities in Washington, D.C., which had been integrated since the end of the Civil War.

May–Oct. 1919 Driven by competition for jobs after World War I, race riots break out in 26 U.S. towns and cities.

June 18, 1936 NAACP attorneys successfully argue that the University of Maryland School of Law must admit a black student because the state does not offer a "separate but equal" law school for blacks.

June 25, 1941 President Franklin D. Roosevelt signs the Fair Employment Act, prohibiting racial discrimination in the defense industry.

Apr. 15, 1947 Jackie Robinson plays for the Brooklyn Dodgers, making him the first African American to play major league baseball in some 60 years.

Jan. 12, 1948 The U.S. Supreme Court rules that the State of Oklahoma and the University of Oklahoma Law School cannot deny admission based on race.

July 26, 1948 President Truman orders the end of segregation in the U.S. military.

1948 The University of Arkansas Law and Medical Schools are integrated without resistance.

Apr. 23, 1951 Black high school students in Farmville, Virginia, go on strike to demand a new school equal in quality to the county's white high schools. The case later becomes part of *Brown v. Board of Education of Topeka, Kansas*.

May 17, 1954 In *Brown v. Board of Education of Topeka, Kansas,* the U.S. Supreme Court rules that "separate but equal" does not apply to public schools, thus overturning *Plessy v. Ferguson.*

May 22, 1954 The Little Rock School Board announces it will comply with the *Brown* ruling.

Aug. 23, 1954 Public schools in Charleston, Arkansas, admit 11 black students, making it the first school district in the former Confederacy to integrate.

Sept. 1954 Seven black students enroll in a formerly all-white high school in Fayetteville, Arkansas.

May 24, 1955 The Little Rock School Board announces its gradual desegregation plan to comply with the *Brown* decision.

May 31, 1955 In *Brown II,* the U.S. Supreme Court rules that desegregation must proceed with "all deliberate speed" as judged by local federal courts.

July 14, 1955 Twenty-one black students peacefully integrate the schools at all levels in Hoxie, Arkansas. Segregationists organize resistance.

Nov. 7, 1955 The Interstate Commerce Commission bans segregation on interstate buses. The U.S. Supreme Court outlaws racial segregation in publicly financed parks, playgrounds, and golf courses.

Dec. 1, 1955 In Montgomery, Alabama, Rosa Parks is arrested for refusing to give up her seat on a bus to a white man. This sparks the Montgomery Bus Boycott, led by Dr. Martin Luther King, Jr., which lasted until December 20, 1956. This resulted in a city ordinance that allowed blacks unrestricted seating on city buses.

Jan. 23, 1956 Daisy Bates leads 27 black students in an attempt to integrate all levels of Little Rock's public schools. They are refused entry because the school district is not ready for integration. On February 8 black parents file a lawsuit in federal court asking that the district integrate without further delay.

Feb. 24, 1956 U.S. Senator Harry F. Byrd, Sr., of Virginia, in response to the *Brown* rulings, announces a campaign of "massive resistance" to prevent school desegregation. The massive resistance strategy quickly spreads throughout the South.

Mar. 11, 1956 Nineteen U.S. Senators and 81 U.S. Representatives sign the Southern Manifesto, calling for reversal of the *Brown* decision.

Apr. 23, 1956 The U.S. Supreme Court bans segregation on intrastate (within state) buses; three days later, Little Rock peacefully integrates its municipal bus system.

Aug. 28, 1956 U.S. District Judge John E. Miller upholds the Little Rock School Board's gradual desegregation plan and rules against the black parents who want immediate integration.

Jan. 1957 The Southern Christian Leadership Council (SCLC), a civil rights group drawing its strength from black churches, is formed, headed by Dr. Martin Luther King, Jr.

Little Rock, 1957–59

Feb. 26, 1957 Governor Faubus of Arkansas signs four school segregation laws passed by the state legislature.

Aug. 29, 1957 In response to a suit filed by Mrs. Clyde Thomason, secretary of the Mothers League of Little Rock Central High School, a local court rules that integration of the school should be delayed because of threats of violence.

Aug. 31, 1957 Newly arrived federal Judge Ronald Davies rules that integration of Central High must proceed.

Sept. 2, 1957 Governor Faubus orders the Arkansas National Guard to surround Central High School.

Sept. 3, 1957 White students attend the first day of school at Central High, while black students stay home at the request of School Superintendent Blossom. In a hearing with the school board, Judge Davies orders integration to proceed the next day.

Sept. 4, 1957 The Little Rock Nine and one other black student attempt to attend Central but are turned away by the National Guard.

Sept. 5–20 The Little Rock Nine remain out of school and work with tutors to keep up with their studies.

Sept. 14, 1957 Governor Faubus meets with President Eisenhower in Newport, Rhode Island, about the crisis.

Sept. 20, 1957 Judge Davies rules that Faubus has used the Guard to interfere with federal integration law rather than to prevent violence. Faubus removes the troops.

pt. 23, 1957 With Little Rock ...ice in charge of security, the ...le Rock Nine enter Central ...h through a side door, while ...angry mob outside attacks ...r black newsmen. Around ...on, Assistant Police Chief ...ne Smith orders the Nine ...noved from the school in ...lice cars.

pt. 24, 1957 Little Rock Mayor ...odrow Mann sends President ...enhower a telegram asking for ...eral troops to maintain order ...d enforce integration. The ...esident sends soldiers of the ...1st Airborne Division to Little ...ck and federalizes the Arkansas ...tional Guard.

pt. 25, 1957 Escorted by ...ldiers of the 101st Airborne, the ...tle Rock Nine enter Central ...gh through the front doors and ...mplete their first full day of ...hool.

t. 1, 1957 The 101st Airborne ...Central High are replaced by ...deralized Arkansas National ...ardsmen. Abuse of the Little ...ck Nine immediately ...creases.

t. 3, 1957 The 101st Airborne ...turns. About 75 white students ...lk out of the school to a ...cant lot where they hang a ...aw dummy of a black student ...m a tree.

v. 1957 The gradual with-...awal of the 101st Airborne is ...mpleted. For the rest of the ...ar, the federalized Arkansas ...tional Guard handles security.

c. 17, 1957 Minnijean Brown ...suspended after dumping chili ...two boys in the cafeteria. She ...turns on January 13, 1958.

b. 6, 1958 After a conflict in ...hich she calls a harasser ...hite trash," Minnijean Brown ...expelled for the rest of the ...hool year.

ay 27, 1958 Ernest Green is the ...st black student to graduate ...m Central High School.

June 21, 1958 Federal District Judge Harry Lemley grants the school board a delay in integrating until January 1961. The NAACP appeals.

Aug. 18, 1958 The Eighth Circuit Court of Appeals reverses the Lemley delay order, and the school board appeals to the U.S. Supreme Court.

Aug. 1958 The state legislature passes a law allowing Faubus to close public schools to avoid integration and to lease the closed schools to private school corporations.

Sept. 12, 1958 The U.S. Supreme Court rules that integration in Little Rock must continue. Governor Faubus orders all four Little Rock high schools closed.

Sept. 16, 1958 A group of white women form the Women's Emergency Committee (WEC) and work to open the schools on an integrated basis.

Sept. 27, 1958 Little Rock voters overwhelmingly oppose integration by a vote of 19,470 to 7,561.

Dec. 6, 1958 A new school board, evenly divided between segregationists and integrationists, is elected.

Mar. 2, 1959 The Little Rock Chamber of Commerce votes in favor of reopening the schools on a plan of minimum integration.

June 1959 The county school board appoints moderates to replace the segregationist members of the Little Rock School Board. The new board announces it will reopen the high schools.

Aug. 12, 1959 Public high schools open. Despite protesters, three black students attend Hall High and three attend Central. It would take until 1972 to integrate all public schools in Little Rock.

Feb. 1, 1960 Four black college students challenge segregation by refusing to leave a lunch counter in Greensboro, North Carolina. This action sparks similar sit-ins throughout the South.

Apr. 1960 Students at Shaw University in North Carolina, the oldest historically black college in the South, create the Student Nonviolent Coordinating Committee (SNCC).

May 4, 1961 The interracial Congress of Racial Equality (CORE) sends seven blacks and six whites on two public buses into the Deep South to test whether the federal ban on segregation of buses and other forms of transportation is being enforced by southern law officers. Severely beaten in Alabama and Mississippi, these "Freedom Riders" inspire other rides as well as protests at train stations and airports.

Nov. 1961 The Interstate Commerce Commission issues new rules prohibiting segregated transportation facilities.

Oct. 1, 1962 James Meredith is the first black student to attend the University of Mississippi.

Aug. 28, 1963 A quarter-million people gather at the Lincoln Memorial to participate in the March on Washington. Martin Luther King, Jr., delivers his "I Have a Dream" speech.

Summer 1964 Thousands of volunteers recruited by the Mississippi Council of Federated Organizations (COFO), which combines efforts of the NAACP, SNCC, and CORE, register black voters.

July 2, 1964 President Lyndon B. Johnson signs the Civil Rights Act of 1964, making it illegal to discriminate in hiring and illegal to segregate public facilities.

Feb. 21, 1965 Malcolm X, leader of the militant Black Muslims, is shot by three gunmen in Harlem, New York.

Mar. 7, 1965 Voting rights marchers are beaten by state troopers in Selma, Alabama.

Aug. 6, 1965 The Voting Rights Act of 1965 outlaws literacy tests used to keep uneducated blacks from voting.

Oct. 6, 1966 The Black Panther Party, a militant self-defense organization, is founded in Oakland, California, by Huey P. Newton and Bobby Seale.

June 12, 1967 The U.S. Supreme Court rules that interracial marriages are legal.

Oct. 2, 1967 Thurgood Marshall becomes the first black U.S. Supreme Court justice.

Apr. 4, 1968 Dr. Martin Luther King, Jr., is shot and killed in Memphis, Tennessee.

Apr. 11, 1968 The Civil Rights Act of 1968 makes it illegal to discriminate in the sale, rental, and financing of housing.

Apr. 20, 1971 The U.S. Supreme Court upholds busing as a legal means for achieving integrated public schools.

Apr. 29, 1992 Race riots erupt in Los Angeles, California, after a jury acquits four white police officers for the videotaped beating of African-American Rodney King.

June 23, 2003 The U.S. Supreme Court rules that race can be one of many factors considered by colleges in selecting students.

Sept. 20, 2007 Some 10 to 20,000 activists gather in Jena, Louisiana, to protest the arrest of six black teenagers who retaliated against white hostility.

Aug. 28, 2008 On the 50th anniversary of Dr. Martin Luther King, Jr.'s "I Have a Dream" speech, Barack Obama becomes the first African American to accept the Democratic Party's nomination for President of the United States.

selected postscripts

The Little Rock Nine received the Congressional Gold Medal in November 1999 in recognition of their contribution to the Civil Rights Movement. They formed the Little Rock Nine Foundation dedicated to promoting racial justice and providing financial support and mentoring to students of color. For more information on the foundation, see: http://www.littlerock9.com

Minnijean Brown (Trickey)* graduated from New Lincoln (High) School in New York and studied journalism at Southern Illinois University. After moving to Canada, she earned bachelor's and master's degrees in social work and worked to protect First Nation (Native American) rights. The subject of the documentary film *Journey to Little Rock*, Mrs. Brown Trickey is an inspirational speaker, diversity consultant, and peace activist.

Elizabeth Eckford returned to Central in August 1959 but discovered she had enough credits to graduate, due to courses she took while the high schools were closed. After attending college for a year, she joined the U.S. Army and later earned a B.A. in history from Central State University in Ohio. After years of struggling with depression, Ms. Eckford has begun to speak out about her experiences. She is a probation officer in Little Rock.

Ernest Green earned a B.S. in social science and an M.S in sociology from Michigan State University. In 1979 he was appointed by President Jimmy Carter as Assistant Secretary of Labor, and in 1993 the Disney Company produced *The Ernest Green Story* based on his experiences at Central. Mr. Green is currently Managing Director of Public Finance for an investment banking firm in Washington, D.C.

* Married names are in parentheses.

continued on p. 60

selected postscripts

continued from p. 59

Thelma Mothershed (Wair) completed high school by correspondence and received her diploma from Central High through the mail. She earned bachelor's and master's degrees from Southern Illinois University and worked as a home economics teacher and guidance counselor in the East St. Louis, Illinois, school system for 28 years. Mrs. Wair now lives in Little Rock.

Melba Pattillo (Beals) completed high school in California. She holds degrees in journalism from San Francisco State and Columbia University and recently earned her Ph.D. Dr. Beals has worked as a television journalist, consultant, speaker, and professor. Her award-winning book,

Warriors Don't Cry, details her experiences at Central High.

Gloria Ray (Karlmark) graduated from a newly integrated high school in Kansas City, Missouri. She earned a B.S. in chemistry and mathematics from the Illinois Institute of Technology and worked as a teacher, mathematician, and patent attorney. After moving to Europe, Mrs. Karlmark founded and served as editor-in-chief of *Computers in Industry.*

Terrence Roberts moved to Los Angeles where he graduated from high school. He earned a B.A. in sociology from California State University Los Angeles, an M.S. in social welfare from UCLA, and a Ph.D in psychology from Southern Illinois University. Dr. Roberts is a practicing psychologist,

professor, motivational speaker, and CEO of a management consultant firm.

Jefferson Thomas graduated from Central High in 1960. He was drafted into the Army in 1965 and served as a staff sergeant in Vietnam. After his service, Mr. Thomas earned a B.A. in Business Administration from Los Angeles State College and became an accountant. In 1978 he went to work for the Department of Defense, retiring in 2004.

Carlotta Walls (LaNier) graduated from Central High in 1960, attended Michigan State for two years, and later completed her bachelor's degree at the University of Northern Colorado. Mrs. LaNier is a real estate broker in Colorado and president of the Little Rock Nine Foundation.

Daisy Bates and her husband were forced to close the *State Press* in October 1959 due to lack of advertising by businesses pressured by segregationists. Mrs. Bates moved to New York and wrote her memoir, *The Long Shadow of Little Rock.* She directed a federal anti-poverty program in Mitchellville, Arkansas. Mrs. Bates died in 1999. Today, a street that runs past Central High School is named Daisy L. Gatson Bates Drive.

Hazel Bryan (Massery) apologized to Elizabeth Eckford in 1963. In 1997 they posed for a series of photos outside of Central High. Both women have spoken publicly about their experiences.

Orval Faubus served a record six consecutive two-year terms as governor of Arkansas.

In 1958 a Gallup poll of the people Americans most admired listed President Eisenhower as #1 and Faubus as #10. His memoir, *Down from the Hills,* was published in 1980. He died in 1994.

Alex Wilson became editor of the *Chicago Defender,* one of America's most prestigious black newspapers, in 1959. Mr. Wilson died in October 1960 from Parkinson's disease caused at least in part by the beating in Little Rock.

Robin Woods (Loucks) never graduated from high school but attended the University of Arkansas in Little Rock based on her SAT scores. She earned degrees in psychology and art and a master's degree in studio art. Mrs. Loucks has owned real estate and catering companies and now lives in Little Rock.

selected sources

Arkansas Democrat,1957–58 (AD)
Arkansas Democrat-Gazette, 1997 (AD-G)
Arkansas Gazette,1957–58 (AG)
Bates, Daisy. *The Long Shadow of Little Rock.* NY: David McKay Co., 1962. Reprint, Fayetteville: The University of Arkansas Press, 1986.
Beals, Melba Pattillo. *Warriors Don't Cry.* NY: Washington Square Press, 1994.
Blossom, Virgil T. *It HAS Happened Here.* NY: Harper & Brothers, 1959.
Brodie, Ralph and Marvin

Schwartz. *Central in Our Lives.* Little Rock: The Butler Center for Arkansas Studies, 2007.
Choosing to Participate: Facing History and Ourselves. Online Module. "Crisis in Little Rock." August 27, 2008. http://ctp.facinghistory.org/ stories/crisis_in_little_rock (CPFHO)
Counts, Will. *A Life Is More Than a Moment.* Bloomington: Indiana University Press, 1999.
Faubus, Orval Eugene. *Down from the Hills.* Little Rock: Pioneer Press, 1980.
Green, Ernest. TV interview, 1962. Little Rock Central

High 40th Anniversary Web site. August 27, 2008. http://www.centralhigh57. org/movie2.htm
Hampton, Henry and Steve Fayer. *Voices of Freedom.* NY: Bantam Books, 1990.
Huckaby, Elizabeth. *Crisis at Central High.* Baton Rouge: Louisiana State University Press, 1980.
Jacoway, Elizabeth. *Turn Away Thy Son.* NY: Free Press, 2007.
Land of Unequal Opportunity. Online Exhibit. University of Arkansas Special Collections. August 27, 2008. http://scipio.uark.edu/ (UARK)

Lewis, Catherine M. and J. Richard Lewis. *Race, Politics, and Memory.* Fayetteville: The University of Arkansas Press, 2007.
Little Rock Central High School National Historic Site. Oral History Project. (NHS)
Little Rock Nine. Speeches during the 50th Anniversary Celebration. Little Rock, AR. September 24–25, 2007. (LR9)
Margolick, David. "Through a Lens, Darkly." *Vanity Fair,* Web exclusive. September 24, 2007.
Reed, Roy. *Faubus.* Fayetteville: The University of Arkansas Press, 1997.

Roberts, Terrence J. "Lessons from Little Rock." (unpublished manuscript)
Roy, Beth. *Bitters in the Honey.* Fayetteville: The University of Arkansas Press, 1999.
Sterling, Dorothy with Donald Gross. *Tender Warriors.* NY: Hill and Wang, 1958.
Stockley, Grif. *Daisy Bates.* Jackson: University Press of Mississippi, 2005.
Walker, Paul Robert. Interviews with multiple participants. (PRW)
Wexler, Sanford. *The Civil Rights Movement.* NY: Facts on File, 1993.

quote sources

Numbers in **bold** refer to page(s) in this book where a quote is found, followed by the speaker, the source identified by author's last name or abbreviation as indicated in parentheses in the bibliography above, and page(s) where quote can be found in the source. Some references are to multiple quotes from a single speaker.

8. Roberts: PRW. **11.** Faubus: *AG* 9/3/57. **11–13.** Eckford: Counts 36–39. **12–16.** Roberts: Roberts. **14.** Bryan: Counts 41. **15.** Lorch: Bates 70. **16–17.** Pattillo: Beals 48–51. **17–18.** Fine: Bates 71. **18.** Burks: UARK; Lorch: Jacoway 6; Marion: Stockley 125. **24.** Johnson: Reed 174; Faubus: Reed 178. **25.** Blossom: Jacoway 57. **26.** Thomason: Jacoway 96; Faubus: Jacoway 97. **27.** Karam: Jacoway 118; Johnson: Reed 213. **28 & 31.**

Black newsman: Bates 92. **29.** Walls: NHS; Eisenhower, *AD* 9/14/57; Eyewitness: Jacoway 156. **30.** Faubus: Jacoway 157. **30–31.** Davies: *AG* 9/21/57. **31.** Mann: *AG* 9/22/57. **32–33.** Wilson: Counts 47–51. **34.** Newspaper: *AG* 9/24/57; Thomason: Lewis 54–55. **35.** Pattillo: Beals 110–111; Woods: Wexler 101; Green: Green TV interview. **36.** Oakley: PRW. **37.** Smith: NHS; Pattillo: Beals 118; Roberts: NHS; Thomas: NHS. **39.** Eisenhower: *AG* 9/24/57.

Green: Wexler 100–101; Mann: Jacoway 176. **40.** Eisenhower: Lewis 60–63; Officer: Bates 104; Bates: CPFHO. **41.** Brown: NHS. **42.** Roberts: Roberts; Eckford: NHS. **43.** Matthews: Huckaby 44; Walker: *AD* 9/25/57; Johnson: NHS; Huckaby: Huckaby 44. **44.** Roberts: NHS; Butler: NHS; Oakes: PRW. **45.** Pattillo & Brown: *AD* 9/26/57. **48.** Pattillo: Beals 148; Eison: *AG-D* 10/5/97. **49.** Panel discussion: Sterling 90–96. **50.** Roberts: NHS;

Mothershed: Hampton 49; Roberts: Roberts; Green: NHS. **51.** Johnson: Brodie 99; Williams: Brodie 31–32; Swafford: Brodie 42. **52.** Eckford: LR9; Brodie: PRW; Matlock: Brodie 29; Brown: PRW. **53.** Gitchel: NHS & PRW; Oakes: Brodie 55. **54.** Brown: PRW; Huckaby: Huckaby 151; Brown: *AG* 2/14/58; Roberts: Roberts; Thomas: NHS; Ray: PRW. **55.** Senior: UARK; Green: NHS.

educational extensions

1. What is the "foreword" of a book? How does a book's foreword add meaning to the text? Read the foreword of *Remember Little Rock* and research its author, Terrence J. Roberts. Why do you think he was chosen to write the foreword? What important background information did you gain about the topic?

2. How does the structure of the text contribute to the meaning and style? Describe the structure of *Remember Little Rock,* including its use of photography, sidebars, and text. Give examples of how the presentation of information enhanced your understanding of the content.

3. In small groups, summarize each chapter and sequence the events that took place in September 1957. Discuss integration as seen from the personal perspectives of different individuals. Distinguish between fact, opinion, and reasoned judgment. Analyze the relationship between primary and secondary sources.

4. Discuss the meaning of "mob rule." Cite textual examples and quotes that discuss mob rule. Are there examples of "mob rule" today?

5. How does the legacy of earlier groups and individuals influence later generations? How would you have acted if you had been a student at Central High in 1957? What life experiences influence your decisions?

more to ponder ...

• Why do authors write nonfiction? How can reading nonfiction shape our ideas, values, beliefs, and behaviors?

• What can we learn from reading real-life accounts of history? How are you affected when reading different points of view? How do the histories of earlier groups and individuals influence later generations?

• How has the world changed from the time period of the text? How do you think it will change in the future?

• Research a topic from the book. Compare and contrast information and details that you found from different sources.